TEN SOUTH

Also by Adam Schwartzman
from Carcanet

The Good Life. The Dirty Life and other stories
Merrie Afrika!

Ten
South African
Poets

edited and introduced by
Adam Schwartzman

CARCANET

First published in Great Britain in 1999 by
Carcanet Press Limited
4th Floor, Conavon Court
12–16 Blackfriars Street
Manchester
M3 5BQ

A CIP catalogue record for this book is available from the British Library.
ISBN 1 85754 393 9

The publisher acknowledges financial assistance
from the Arts Council of England.

Set in Stempel Garamond by XL Publishing Services, Tiverton
Printed and bound in England by SRP Ltd, Exeter

Contents and Biographical Notes

ARTHUR NORTJE Born in Oudtshoorn, Western Cape, in
1942. At Patterson High School, Port Elizabeth, he was greatly
influenced by his English teacher, Dennis Brutus. He went on
to the University of the Western Cape and Jesus College,
Oxford. After two years of teaching in Canada, he returned to
Oxford in 1970, dying the same year of an overdose of barbi-
turates. His poetry is collected in two posthumous volumes,
Lonely Against the Light and *Dead Roots*, both published in
1973.

MONGANE WALLY SEROTE Born in 1944 in Sophiatown,
a township within the Johannesburg area, since destroyed. In
1969 he spent nine months in solitary confinement but was
released without being charged. In 1979 he studied at the
University of Columbia, then went to work at the Medu Arts
Ensemble in Gaberone, Botswana. He began working for the
Department of Arts and Culture at the UK office of the African
National Congress in 1986. He is currently an MP and head of
the ANC Department of Arts and Culture in Johannesburg. His

poetry was pivotal in the revival of black writing in the 1970s. His collections include *Yakhal 'iinkomo* (1972) and *Tselo* (1974); five long poems published in book form include *No Baby Must Weep* (1975) and *Come Hope with Me* (1993).

MAFIKA GWALA   Born in Verulam, Natal, in 1946. Among other occupations, he has worked as an industrial-relations officer among black workers in the Hammarsdale area. In the early 1970s he was a leading exponent of the Black Consciousness Movement, and in 1987 went to the University of Manchester to study politics and labour relations. He was a founding member of the Mpumalanga Arts Ensemble. His literary output includes numerous critical articles and essays as well as two volumes of poetry: *Jol'iinkomo* (1977) and *No More Lullabies* (1982). In 1991 he collaborated with Liz Gunner in editing and translating a selection of Zulu praise poems, *Musho*.

WOPKO JENSMA   Born in Ventersdorp, Transvaal, in 1939; he went to the universities of Pretoria and Potchefstroom. He lived in Mozambique and worked as a teacher and graphic artist for the Botswana Information Department before returning to South Africa in 1971. For personal reasons, he took the unusual step of having himself reclassified as black. In recent years he has been in and out of psychiatric hospitals. His three volumes of poetry include work in English and Afrikaans, with snippets of Tswana and other languages, as well as woodcuts and collages. They are *Sing for Our Execution* (1973), *Where White is the Colour, Where Black is the Number* (1974) and *I Must Show You My Clippings* (1977).

DOUGLAS LIVINGSTONE   Born in Kuala Lumpur, Malaysia, in 1932, he arrived in South Africa at the age of ten. He trained as a bacteriologist in Southern Rhodesia and settled in Durban in 1964, where he worked as a consultant microbiologist on the question of sea pollution. He is the author of three radio plays and two books of translation. His seven volumes of poetry are *The Skull in the Mud* (1960), *Sjambok and Other Poems from Africa* (1964), *Poems* (with Thomas Kinsella and Anne Sexton, 1968), *Eyes Closed Against the Sun* (1970), *A Rosary of Bone* (1975), *The Anvil's Undertone* (1978), *A Littoral Zone* (1991). His *Selected Poems* were published in 1984. He died in 1996.

LIONEL ABRAHAMS Born in Johannesburg in 1928. He was
mentored by the writer Herman Charles Bosman, whose uncol-
lected work he began editing in 1953. He launched the now
defunct magazine *Purple Renoster* in 1957, and under the
Renoster Books imprint published the debut volumes of
Oswald Mtshali and Wally Serote in the early 1970s. Between
1977 and 1981 he became one of the 'fifth columnists for stan-
dards' within the South African branch of PEN. Since 1975 he
has run a series of poetry workshops. He has published a collec-
tion of autobiographical stories, *The Celibacy of Felix
Greenspan* (1977). His poetry collections are: *Thresholds of
Tolerance* (1975), *Journal of a New Man* (1984), *The Writer in
Sand* (1988) and *A Dead Tree Full of Live Birds* (1995). A selec-
tion of his writings is available in *Lionel Abrahams: A Reader*
(1988).

INGRID DE KOK Born in Johannesburg in 1951, she grew up
in Stilfontein, a mining town in the Western Transvaal. She
studied in South Africa and Canada, and directs the Department
of Adult Education and Extra Mural Studies at the University
of Cape Town. She co-edited *Spring Is Rebellious: Arguments
about Cultural Freedom* (1990) and was advisory editor for the
World Literature Today issue on South African literature (1996).
Her two volumes of poetry are *Familiar Ground* (1988) and
Transfer (1997).

TATAMKHULU AFRIKA Born in Sollum, Egypt, in 1920,
the son of an Arab father and a Turkish mother, he was brought
to South Africa in 1923. He was a prisoner of war for three years

in Italy and Germany, after which he worked on and off for twenty years in the Namibian copper mines. He settled in Cape Town in the 1960s and converted to Islam. He founded the organisation Al-Jihaad that was active during the uprising against the apartheid government when it declared District Six a white area. Arrested again in 1987 for 'terrorism', he was listed for five years as a banned person. He has published two novels and a collection of novellas. His six books of poetry are *Nine Lives* (1991), *Dark Rider* (1992), *Maqabane* (1994), *The Lemon Tree* (1995), *Flesh and Flame* (1995) and *Turning Points* (1996).

KAREN PRESS Born in Cape Town in 1956, she has worked in alternative education projects, helped to found a publishing collective, and is employed as an editor of fiction for young adults. She co-edited *Spring Is Rebellious: Arguments about Cultural Freedom* (1990). She has also published several stories, and five collections of poetry: *This Winter Coming* (1986), *Bird Heart Stoning the Sea* (1990), *History is the Dispossession of the Heart* (1992), *The Coffe Shop Poems* (1993) and *Eyes Closed Against the Sun* (1997).

SEITLHAMO MOTSAPI Born in 1966 in Bela Bela, a town-ship outside Warmbaths in the Northern Transvaal. He studied at the University of the Witwatersrand and the University of the North, where he went on to lecture in English. His first volume of poetry, *earthstepper / the ocean is very deep*, was published in 1995.

Introduction

i

The purpose of this anthology is to make available to an international readership a substantial selection from the work of each of ten South African poets. To bring together substantial selections I have had to set a limit to the number of poets represented in these pages. This is the reason for my selection of *only* ten. Many of South Africa's finest poets have not written in English, but I have confined my selection to those who have. A collection of South African poetry in translation is a project deserving of its own anthology. The earliest poems collected here were written four decades ago; the most recent are contemporary. Just under four decades ago, in 1960, the ANC and PAC were banned, and crowds protesting against the pass laws were shot down in Sharpeville. Within a year the armed wings of the resistance movements had been founded. This then would seem one plausible water-shed beyond which South Africa was another country, an intuitive marker – political as well as cultural (for art and politics have been exceptionally closely linked in South Africa, as in the rest of Africa) – for the beginning of the 'recent past'.

In 1973 a special edition of the South African poetry magazine, *New Coin*, was devoted to the work of Arthur Nortje. Nortje had died in exile, of a drugs overdose, three years earlier. The magazine contained the following reminiscence by the South African writer Richard Rive:

> In 1966 I was returning from the United States and spending a few days in London, when Albert Adams, the painter, asked me whether I knew Arthur Nortje. I was surprised and pleased to hear that he was now at Oxford reading English. And then a few years after that I read in a newspaper that he was dead.
>
> I once received a seventeen page letter from a person I had never heard of before. His name was Pascal Gwala and he was a poet from Durban. In the letter he gave what was for me a

brilliant analysis of the South African literary situation, and amongst other things he wrote:

> Death is a process and therefore very much relative and objective. Death does not begin with the last pulse of the heartbeat. Neither does it end with the doctor's certificate. Death can be said to begin when a person's will fails to identify itself with life. And will is such a vastness of violent possibilities that to try to understand it we are always pressed on to the understanding of environment first.

And I remember on a sunny morning I was working at my desk in Cape Town, and the phone rang and Margery was on the phone and she cried and told me that Ingrid Jonker was dead. Another poet dead. Did her will fail to identify itself with life?

And I also remember I wrote a long letter to Nat Nakasa and told him to shake out of his depression, that I was coming over to study in America and within weeks I would see him and we would laugh and talk and argue about literature. But he couldn't wait and threw himself from a building in New York before I came. Did he not understand his environment first?

And then I read in a newspaper that Arthur Nortje was dead. When I went up to Oxford I asked others about him. Some said he was depressed and was an introvert, others said he sat in a pub and wouldn't speak, but read Dickens. And others were even more vague. Then a friend of his came up to read poetry at Ruskin, and before he read he told us about Arthur, and I learnt that he had severed and not severed his ties, that his passport had expired, that he took drugs, that he faced deportation. Then I knew what he meant when he wrote:

> Night after night I lie and wait
> for sleep's return, but she, but she,
> is gripped in spastic fits of fear,
> trembling at noises made by me.

There is no more to say. So little remains, so little to tell. Maybe its best to stop, sufficient to know that he still is, Arthur Nortje – Poet.

Of course there are many senses in which 'Arthur Nortje – Poet' is all a poet needs to be. Poems, we say, decide for themselves how they are to be read. But it is equally true that they do not appeal to readers in empty spaces. They are – among many other things – intricate social interactions. They are objects of art the meanings of which are crafted out of lived realities that are the pre-conditions of both their composition, and – in a different way – of the reader's ability to engage with them. *The will is such a vastness of violent possibilities*, says Gwala, *that to try to understand it we are always pressed on to the understanding of environment first.*

This is not to insist that South African poetry has to be read in *a* particular way. South Africans may want to be Africans or African*ists* or citizens of the world, they may choose to hunt their private lives, they are men and women, workers, activists and academics and all the other things that a person living in South Africa might be, and in terms of which the poems may be read. Nor is this to say that 'environment' serves in any way to justify these poems. The only justification for a poem is what it does with words. Rather it is to insist on a heightened sensitivity to the commitments that such poems make, and attention to the material out of which they are made – to the postures invoked, the debates engaged, the somersaults turned and in whose language, the fun prodded, the gesture celebrated, satirised, despaired in, or made light of.

In compiling this anthology I have been drawn in particular to poems that, in sensing the world, remake it. This happens when poets do something fascinating and invigorating through language. They are able to do it because they find compelling ways of engaging with the world. There is an important sense in which these kinds of poems are poems that 'embrace their own origins'. The phrase is Maurice Merleau-Ponty's, and this is what he means by it: 'The artist', he says,

launches his work just as a man once launched the first word, not knowing whether it will be anything more than a shout, whether it can detach itself from the flow of individual life in which it was born and give the independent existence of an identifiable meaning to the future of that same individual life, or to the monads coexisting within it, or the open community of future monads. The meaning of what the artist is going to say does not exist anywhere – not in things, which as yet have no meaning, nor in the artist himself, in his unformulated life. It summons one away from the already constituted reason in which 'cultured men' are content to shut themselves, toward a reason which would embrace its own origin.

A final word on my responsibilities as an anthologist, in partic-
ular as an anthologist in a country in which the struggle over
collective identity is as fiercely contested as it is: the responsibili-
ties of the anthologist are different from those of the poet. The
poet has no responsibility other than to make wonderful, engaging
poems (which, of course, may or may not meet the criteria for any
particular reader's notion of 'wonderful, engaging poems'). But
anyone who compiles an anthology for publication acts as a gate-
keeper to the public realm. There are many ways in which the
anthologist might respond to the social responsibility that he or
she therefore incurs. The criteria of strict representationality
appropriate to the survey anthology is but one. This anthology is
different in kind. It has been compiled in the spirit that its respon-
sibility can equally be met by developing and promoting critical
sensibilities that cut across and negate the various sets of exclusive
and intolerant notions in South Africa of what constitutes the
poetic, as it can by accepting these terms, and attempting an 'impar-
tial' selection. I have tried to compile an anthology that rises to the
example set by the poets I have collected, one that dispenses with
the 'already constituted reason' of cultured men and women. The
legacies of so many old critical projects – those, for instance, of
growing a western poetry in African soil, or of turning poetry *solely*
into a weapon of struggle – weigh today like a nightmare on the
consciousness of the living (to invoke Marx). The living have their
own choices to make, and this anthology represents one of many
such sets of choices. It is the choice of a particular moment, by a
particular person. I hope that I do not inhabit my sense of that
moment on my own. It is my hope that many readers in and outside
of South Africa will be able to share in it. This, then, is *my* reason
for compiling this anthology.

ii

Arthur Nortje is a theatrical poet. He passes mirrors. He points,
to himself and other poems. He chooses to place himself on a stage.
He is intensely aware of his relationship with his reader, *as a poet*.
He makes elaborate gestures, appeals to us in intricate rhetorical
strategies and conceits. Throughout he is intensely aware that he
is a person *experiencing*.

By 1967 Nortje was in literal exile. *Literal* exile because already,
through his engagement with the experience of 1960s South Africa

– ravaged by bannings, arrests and forced removals – he had made the language of displacement, estrangement and isolation his own. In 'Hangover', the first of the four early poems collected here, escape has already 'become the fashion', the condition that would characterise Nortje's poetry and his life. The poem itself goes underground, checking and censoring itself. The details that make the passing of time particular and specific, become as fugitive as the people who have experienced them. The poem is made of oddments – bits and pieces 'blindly remembered' – snatched from a disappearing world. The smallest of happenings – damage done by a football kicked indoors, a man asleep protecting his wallet – are lost, turned into shadows and echoes, as if they too have been banned. Nortje's precocious development (some of these poems were written by a twenty-three-year-old), coincides with the banning of the very eloquence he was learning. In 'Soliloquy: South Africa' the freedom to give and receive love becomes subversive. Love poems become monologues. Who can I be, these early poems seem to ask, when cut off from the repositories of identity that guarantee me more than a bare existence, when speech itself, the means by which as a poet I make myself, is buried?

In later years Nortje's question becomes 'What can credibly save me?' Many of these poems take up as their themes the loneliness of exile, both personal and existential, the poet's increasingly self-destructive tendencies, self-loathing, aspects too of the struggle and the anxieties of 'coloured' identity.[1] Nortje writes out of a sense of a growing desolation. He is the man to whom nothing belongs. He plummets through his poems like a man falling from the sky, unable to grab onto anything. His self portrait, in 'Reflections in a passing mirror', is a fleeting image made of disconnected pieces, fragments – in the Eliotesque sense – shored up against a ruin: the artefacts of lost cultures, splinters of mammoth bone, remembered pieces of a literature, lonely, fleeting visions of nature, the hectic, disorientated interior of a club. In 'Night ferry' the body endures and suffers its passage through time, its removal from origins, from even the tropes of those poems of travel and movement that once expressed exile – from the whale and the wolf and the albatross.

In these later poems distilling loneliness itself into poetry –

1　In South Africa the term 'coloured' refers to people of racially mixed decent. It was part of the apartheid system of race classification, and was to be distinguished from the terms 'white', 'Indian' and 'black'. Large sections of the 'coloured' communities are Afrikaans speaking. Although contested, it is not a term of abuse.

'keening on the blue strings of the blood' (perhaps as Rimbaud plays his bootstrings like a lyre) – is loneliness's only compensation, the salt of victory slaved away for in the Siberia of 'Native's letter'. Against the backdrop of exile, Nortje reaches out for those sharp, exquisite intensities of sensations out of which he makes his poem. The process – like the image itself with which it is described in 'Waiting' – is of turning meaning further and further inwards: the poem is like a phosphorescent fish; the fish is acute as a glittering nerve; one metaphor defers to another, experience is taken further and further inwards, absorbed into the inner life.

But the process of distillation brings him no closer to resolution, 'to anything affectionate'. Acts of fulfilment are transitory at the moment they are experienced. The final image of 'Episodes with unusables' bursts into life at the moment it makes explicit the failure to regenerate:

> We have not seen
> the patience of waiting the seeds suffered,
> the weathers they withstood in their infinite wisdom,
> the tiny roots that felt their way into life,
> the tendrils that clung.
> Your hair fell over my eyes,
> your aching beauty held me rooted.

Out of a struggle against a similar state of despair, a new group of poets in the 1970s crafts its aesthetics. Nortje's 'What can credibly save me?' becomes in the times of high apartheid, Gwala's *How do I maintain the will to identify with life*? – a question to which the Black Consciousness thinkers and poets formulated a resounding answer. Black Consciousness was above all an effort of self-creation, a conscious, collective effort of re-invention. By the mid-1960s large-scale popular black resistance to Apartheid had been crushed. A new generation grew up cut off from the revolutionary tradition of the 1940s and 1950s, which had channelled the revolutionary initiative into 'multi-racialism', and which the repression of the 1960s brought to an end. The cut-off was not total, nor did Black Consciousness represent a complete break with the past; it was a manifestation of one strand that was always present in the tradition of black resistance. The effects of Black Consciousness were not universal, but it did provide a radical and, especially for the young, an attractive and powerful vocabulary in which they *might* articulate their predicament, a new set of metaphors with which to organise the imaginative confrontation with political oppression.

The poet of *No Baby Must Weep* – a poem of some thousand lines of which I reprint sections here – stands like the magician in Walt Disney's *Fantasia*, who fills with life a previously inanimate world, that whirls around him at the borders of his control, that he struggles to master, and that he finally sweeps together into the apotheosis of the last line: 'ah/africa/is this not your child come home'. The poets who write in the spirit of Black Consciousness ideals do not have the luxury of an aesthetic vocabulary immediately to hand and therefore have to work for it in order to articulate that 'vague fever' which precedes the making of art. These poems convey us on a journey in which charting a path, and following it, are simultaneous; a journey that – like the jazz improvisation – consists of the very acts of self-creation that bring it into existence. It is a poetry that constantly makes its own dangers and takes its own chances (thus Stanley Cavel describes the conditions under which all genuinely new art succeeds), that 'reins its own horses for solving problems'. *No Baby Must Weep* travels through a series of metaphors and bundles of images, playing with them, spinning the poem out of them, then modulating one into the next, merging each revision into the fabric of the poem without going back on itself (the hallmark of performance). The insistent repetitions and refrains that hold these texts together give them an extraordinary declamatory force. They run the reader down, thriving on the mind's struggle to process them at a reading.

The language of which many of these poems are made – the fast-living, loving, drinking, dying language of township and town – is fantastically vibrant, and a resource on which the poets constantly draw. In Gwala's 'Bonk'abajahile', for instance:

> Playboy Joe was already at Umgababa
> pulling dagga zol with other majitas

The slightest inflections often invest a simple language with great agility: streets groan, footsteps are hasty and running, there are 'loads' of them in Serote's 'Night-time'; but fixed into a syntax that constantly unsettles, the effect is powerful:

> tomorrow the streets will groan with loads of footsteps,
> hasty footsteps
> running footsteps
> hurrying to play hide and seek with dignity in the city,
> inside the skyscrapers, where a breath is held.

At the same time these poems invoke one distinct South African literary language; that of a racy journalistic prose that marks so much writing, especially of the 1950s. It revels in its sensationalism, and does so with an energy that makes it possible again to use the English language to wield, without irony, such phrases as these:

> Bongi Ndlovu
> She tried to run, to flee, to plead;
> Whick! Whack!
> Into flesh came the bushknife
> On the sand dunes she collapsed
> Waiting for fate to say it's over;
> How she let her soul go
> is a mystery to bemoan.

The semantic forms into which this language falls, however, are as hard and material as the worlds out of which they are dragged. These poems are forceful expressions of anger. They struggle to maintain the will to identify with life in something of the terms in which that struggle is lived: the metaphors are sparse, saying no more than they need, for these poems are not 'adorned objects'. But while they employ a rhetoric of struggle, jaded by the grim uniformity of suffering, they do so in a way that gives the lie to the notion that this rhetoric is unreflexive: the brothers who, in Gwala's 'Getting off the ride', are waiting on the dark street corners, who are sent to mental asylum, who are forced into exile, are also the brothers who 'bullshit me for a Rand', who'll roll their fathers on a Friday night.

In the introduction to the first edition of Aimé Césaire's *Cahier d'un retour au pays natal*, André Breton argues that Césaire's book derives its supreme value from a certain 'power of transformation',

> which consists in taking the most discredited materials, among which daily squalor and constraints, ultimately producing neither gold nor the philosophers stone any longer but freedom itself.

This is no less true of the radical South African poetry of the 1970s and early 1980s. Sometimes the transformation is turned into a strategy for structuring a poem: Gwala's 'Beyond fences' is one such poem of transformation, of imaginative escape from a confounding reality, with its shifts in vocabulary and register that, across verse paragraphs, turns weakness into strength, flight from the police into imaginative empowerment. The strategy is similar at the end of 'Getting off the ride', with its breaking from the language of political confrontation and the rhetoric of analysis and denunciation into ritual and chant. It is achieved with neither affectation nor 'naiveté'. It is the conscious drawing of a particular resource into a carefully created context, the effect of which is more than artistic justification:

> I hear the sound of African drums beating
> to freedom songs;
> And the sounds of the Voice come:
>   Kungu, Kungu!
>   Untshu, Untshu!
>   Funtu, Funtu!
>   Shundu, Shundu!
>   Sinki, Sinki!
>   Mojo, Mojo!
> O-m! O—o—m! O—-hhhhhhhhhmmmm!!!

The kinds of freedom to which these poems aspire are not only a matter of making art out of a world of degradation and oppression. The poems derive from an explicit commitment to transform the reality that they and their audiences inhabit. These are poems, as Breton remarked of the *Cahier*, with explicit theses. Often they are working objects. They are tools for consciousness-raising. Much of the force of Gwala's 'Getting off the ride', for instance, comes out of its commitment to *compel* the reader into understanding. He does this in part through the clarity with which he is alive to his predicament, and his stark understanding of its mechanics. He does this through his piling on of the details of his world and the characters who people it, in flurries of striking images: the naked boy running down a muddy road, the pipeskyf pulling cat, the skhotheni who confronts the devileyed police, the young tsotsi found murdered in a donga in the unlit streets of Edendale, Mdantsane, the voluntarily scruffy (white) hippie and market woman, scruffy through compulsion. He does this with an unflagging, angry energy that is intoxicating, in the way that the energy of large crowds is intoxicating.

Wopko Jensma's outlook is no less radical than that of the Black Consciousness writers. Although his work is not political in any overt sense, it is perhaps here – in three books of poems published between 1973 and 1977 – that the most 'transformative' and revolutionary gestures of the decade are to be found.

Like many radical writers from Afrikaans backgrounds in the 1970s, his orientation was, if toward anywhere outside of South Africa, toward Europe, not England or America. The influence of his interest in Dada, and his association through the small South African literary magazine, *Wurm*, with the Flemish and Dutch avante-garde of the day can be felt in his work. So too can the chronic schizophrenia from which he suffered. In his poems, as in his woodcuts and collages, Jensma bends the world into extraordinary, often grotesque and harsh forms. Many of his poems deny the constraints of the real through parody and ironic transformation, exploding the very structures that make reality possible. 'Now is not the time to cry' one suspect tells another in 'Suspect under section a1 appeal' and twists into subversive farce the language of medico-bureaucratic officialdom; in doing so, he strips it of its power:

> sobs stations stick like, hey
> lyster 'k sê: 'patients are advised to remain
> standing while the lift motions passengers to drop
> teatrays' – a-one, a-two, a-three! dis curry-'n-ruti!

To enter Jensma's poems is often like waking up blind-folded, hearing voices, snatched phrases, disembodied conversation, from which alone one has to deduce where one is. His poems implicate us in their processes of transformation, insisting on our participation in the realisation of the crazy, undone liberated world of the poet; in the construction out of shards of conversation, snippets of detail, dashes of idiom, scenes and views from a world we have the information to understand, but lack the instructions to realise – a lack which the poem itself satisfies. Welcome to the place I inhabit, Jensma seems to say, the world of 1970s South Africa and Mozambique, a world in the grip of grand apartheid, teetering towards anarchy, wild with the permutations of a hundred different life-worlds, in which Sesotho, English, Afrikaans, Portuguese, Dutch and dialects of each, swirl around each other. It is a world characterised by brutal exoticism, impotence, vibrancy, and fantastical tragi-comic suffering:

> mr noah von ark's shady carnival
> mrs von ark's soft lined fur
>   say-say say't
>   o say't now
>
> *amakaladi*:   tjarra, tjarra ad infinitum

kaffir: amaboen, amaboen, ad infinitum
amaboen: kaffir, kaffir ad infinitum
tjarra: amakaladi-ladiii ad infinitum
curryball: a-hmm sanctus dominus dei
                     : *ad lib all together now*

amatjrblackaf bludybalshiterboenwhitrock

    afs are great!
    porras are nice!
now that we hate, that we once loved
but what about our children?

yr exposure to our wonderful people
our cool climate: best in the world!
    sumthin, yes's
    sumthin bout'm
                ('The pointless objects riddle')

An insistence on humanity in the teeth of a state apparatus that would deny it runs through all the poems in this anthology. For Jensma however, more so than for Gwala or Nortje, the effort of carving an identity out of one's surroundings is as much an existential problem as a struggle against oppression. It is also more explicitly tied up with the effort of writing poetry, of *being a poet*: 'i hope to leave some evidence/that i inhabited this world', Jensma says in 'Spanner in the what? works',

    that i sensed my situation
    that i created something
    out of my situation
    out of my life
    that i lived
    as human
    alive
    i

This is precisely what Jensma achieves: through his extraordinary poetic idiom, with its distinctive rhetorical strategies and its innovative textures; through his constant evasion of literary authority; his mastery of social idioms; his suspension in all kinds of ways of the readers' confidence that he or she is being addressed as the reader of a poem; through his challenge to the reader to become conscious of how he or she is being brought into the creation of the poem; and above all through his insistence that the reader *understand* (perform that gesture of empathy in understanding) the world out of which he writes.

It is not until the appearance of the work of Press and Motsapi in the late 1980s and 1990s, that we again hear voices that resonate with anything like the same imaginative energies as those of the poets of the 1970s. Almost two decades, however, will have passed. The decaying Apartheid state has, since the mid-1980s, become desperate and ferocious in its brutality. State sponsored and revolutionary violence has reached terrifying intensities. The most powerful voices to emerge as the new dispensation drew near are blasted of both innocence and optimism. This does not preclude a certain kind of light-heartedness. Karen Press's fourth book, *Coffee Shop Poems*, comprises a series of pastiches; reviews of Cape Town restaurants run along the foot of each page of her fifth, *Echo Location;* but rarely does this light-heartedness share the same arena with those poems that respond to the immediate realities of the 1990s.

Press's most striking pieces are guarded, drained of celebratory instinct, uninterested in the brilliant details of the everyday. Often ironic, they have little faith or expectation of redemption. These are poems made out of the *failure* of the will to identify with life. The imaginary spaces into which she projects her voice are, unlike those of Jensma, hostile and estranging. Mythical landscapes, denuded and ruined, are traversed by anonymous suffering, as suffering has become in South Africa by virtue of its repetitive enormity. They are often full of distinct experiences – experiences however, that are generic; however specific their details become, they do not belong to a particular 'real' person, but to a community of experience: forced removal, urbanisation, political struggle.

Press takes up these mythologised themes in a way that refuses to turn them into *mere* political icons, although political icons they inevitably are: 'In Sharpeville your arms died', says the figure of Tiresias, speaking as a brutalised freedom fighter, refusing to tell the story of the war in which 'each of us became the nation':

In Uitenhage your tongues died.
In Boipatong your eyes died.
In Katlehong and Bekkersdal and Empangeni you died and
                                  you died and you died.
That's what I remember.

The huge social processes that take place in her poems draw around them the imagery of the body and the natural world in a way suggestive of dreams. Many of her poems turn on the experience of disembodied subjectivity in which real events and objects are manipulated into unreal situations, to reflect back on the experientially 'true' nature of the real.

As in the work of Nortje, although differently refracted, the figure of the wanderer drifts through Press's poems: the destitute market woman wandering in the city's dreamscapes; the body stripped of its cells and atoms as it lies down to rest; the city itself, that meta-unit of identity, which finds itself robbed of its own identity by those who tussle over it to secure their own:

> All people live in my home and say it is not me, it is not,
> all people invite me in and say look, it is not yours, welcome.
>
> Any person has permission because of history.
> Because of justice. Because of songs of genesis.
> Any person being decidedly here in my self
>   banishes me. Any person refuses permission.
> Any person who says nothing, or everything,
> does not say my name. Any person is here in my place
> it is not my place.

In the imaginary worlds that she creates, Press characteristically casts herself in the role of the witness. In his, Seitlhamo Motsapi casts himself as the herald. Motsapi's 'samaki' is a naming poem, a calling into existence of the world. The water that 'holler[s] us welcome' is more than the water out of which, in some general sense, all life is made. It is also the receding waters of the flood, the retreat of which makes possible the recreation of life anew. And it is life *anew*. If, as Kwame Anthony Appiah has argued, the project of (Pan-) Africanist literary culture has in the past been dominated by a *search for* culture, implicitly defined against some European norm, Seitlhamo Motsapi is the first South African poet writing in the Africanist tradition for whom this ceases to be so. Identity, for Motsapi, is no longer a posture of defence, nor an ideological shell. To invoke the terms of Wole Soyinka's memorable polemic, Motsapi writes from a position of 'culture-security', *taking for granted* the African worlds out of which the poem is created.

Motsapi does not write from the perspective of any of those elites which, in the process of decolonisation, have so often taken it upon themselves to broker cultural identities on the behalf of those they purport to represent. He insists on defining 'we' from below, out of popular forms of culture. The language of his poems rings with the inflections of the bus-station, the street-corner, the spaza-shop, the tavern after sunset, and of Africa's pervasive rasta-farian culture. It includes the voice of pulpit, of cell meeting and political rally – messianic, apocalyptic, demotic, at once deeply religious and political in its wielding of the heavy units of utopi-anism. Yet the distinctive, potentially overbearing vocabularies that Motsapi uses never reduce the poems to their own particular logics. The units out of which 'sol/o' is made are extremely bold but the effect of the poem is anything but that of sham-profundity or sentimentality. Rather we are arrested by images that are powerful, complex and daring in their assemblage. The different journeys on which we are taken in unravelling the metaphors of the penultimate verse-paragraph, for instance, are not a weakness, but a consummate strength:

> i tell u this
> as the sun recedes
> into the quaking pinstripe
> of my warriors
> grinning & vulgar in their muddied dreams
> of power

Seitlhamo Motsapi does not turn English into an African language; he uses it in ways that show that it has already achieved that status. His poems emphatically deny Ngugi wa Thiongo's claim that African literature can only be written in African languages.

The 'culture security' out of which Motsapi writes has little to do, then, with the essentialist gestures of early Africanism. His poems acknowledge all kinds of negotiated and contested forms of culture, which they celebrate. But they do more than celebrate; they are 'carnivalesque': in the carnival crowd, says Bakhtin, the individual 'is aware of being a member of a continually growing and renewed people', shifting, seething, continually rejecting new forms of hegemony, their chief modes of resistance, parody and laughter. The first section of 'djeni', for instance, shakes apart the character of the 'new man', taking up and parodying the pseudo-New-World-Order rhetoric that soon degenerates into high-modern stereotypes, with its cut-out figures from the text-books of colonial anthropology virtually unchanged. The poem slips in and out of different levels of meaning: at first uncritically summoning up the character of the 'new man', then exposing through parody what it shows to be no more than the invention of a new bogus rhetoric, denouncing the realities that lie behind the stereotypes, and finally satirising a state of affairs in which it is possible for a Western pop-icon to shuttle out with a TV crew to save those who are helpless to save themselves, which only confirms these stereotypes to the receivers of these television images.

For many South African poets inside and outside the Africanist tradition making poetry can be described as a 'compulsive cultural act', as Es'kia Mphahlele suggests. One pauses before applying this term to the work of Douglas Livingstone – partly because of the distance the poems maintain from the political and social issues that have defined South African cultural life, and partly because much of his writing is playful and gracious in ways that deny any notion of 'compulsion'.

Until his death in 1996 Douglas Livingstone was frequently described as South Africa's greatest living poet. His poems can be sparklingly intelligent and agile, ready-witted and eloquent; often they are elusive jokes, content to be what they are, refusing to yield to the reader; at the same time they can be brooding and contemplative – a combination of the mercurial and saturnine, to use the terms Livingstone sets out in 'One Golgotha'.

Livingstone is often described as a latter-day Romantic: the lover of the land, the ecologist. But a figure of enlightenment wit seems to me equally, and sometimes more appropriately, to fit him. (His love of the land, after all, is a *scientist's* love.) Livingstone takes as his point of departure not the private life or the social life but the human condition. The nocturnal terrorisms that stalk through 'A Darwinian preface' are not immediately those of the assassination squad, but those inherent in the fact of being alive. The body is caught up in vortexes and cycles; life winds and unwinds itself around the twisted strands of DNA; the body takes part in continual journeys, is made up of journeys, is finally shaken toward death. The world Livingstone chooses to describe hums and throbs with natural processes – processes that are not imbued with any moral value, even if they result in terror. They are simply the processes of being part of the natural world; and the natural world is indifferent to human happiness or suffering. The only truth to be distilled from experience, says the old fisherman in 'Sonatina of Peter Govender, beached' is that 'Contempt for death is the hard-won/ultimate, the only freedom'. This is Livingstone at his darkest and most Byronic. His outlook is more characteristically stoical: the concluding words of 'A Darwinian preface' – 'Best buckle to' – are an appropriate measure.

The Littoral Zone (1992) was Livingstone's final book. After a poetic silence of thirteen years he began for the first time – in poems like 'The waste land at Station 14' and 'Decent from the tower' – to touch on some of the issues that other poets in this anthology deal with directly. 'The waste land at Station 14', perhaps the most important South African poem in English about writing in a state of emergency, is Livingstone's answer to the relevance/standards debate. It denounces its sterility, but at the same time acknowledges the then present inability to transcend its terms, the impossibility of writing a poetry that glories in the world when the people who inhabit it are so brutally housed; and when the poet, too, untouched by its madness, cannot yet exist. To the 'political' performance poet Shozi Bengu, he writes

5

Under Africa's moon there dreams a strand
older than old the ancient poets keep.
We both walk it under Africa's sun.
There, a glad profusion of brow and hand
– struck from one Mind – strikes deeper than the one
hundred or so microns which spell skin-deep;
where we could wake those old ones from their sleep
with such poems we have not yet begun
to sing: the love which Africa has fanned,
to hymn the earth perhaps, something as grand.

6

Brother-poet, verbose and gallant,
I mourn the sands that waste our talent.

As distinctive in its commitments is the work of Lionel Abrahams. Poet, novelist, critic, essayist, publisher and editor, Abrahams has played a defining and not uncontroversial role in South African letters of the last thirty-five years. He was instrumental in nurturing and promoting the work of Serote and Oswald Mtshali, yet his own poems – the first of which were published in book form during that same period – could not be more different in outlook. Of the poets collected here, he has most in common with Livingstone – not in the texture of the poems themselves, but in the way they position themselves. Here is the conclusion of Abrahams' 'The Mortality of planets', dedicated to Livingstone:

Promising no salvation,
firm to his faith in facts, he dares

enjoin us: Love each other, love the planets,
read the poets more.

The literate heart lifts-off toward
this tender, vigilant alchemist of words
whose science and vision prove
his resurrecting name –
protector of living waters,
living stone.

Abrahams is urban, metropolitan, cerebral, erudite. He is
possessed too of an unflinching integrity and humility that fore-
close the possibility of factitious wit or academicism or any subtle
form of fraudulence. He is also the South African poet least defined
by the place in which he happens to live. What he identifies with,
what makes him who he is, is not a community of experience, but
ideas and values, independent of contingency. He declares himself
'Born but never Native here', heir not to a land and community,
but to 'the Book', his only 'prospect of a self-built meaning'
residing on 'second generation strangers'. The truths he extols are
not *embodied* in the land, or in place or in a community, but are
rational and abstract, systematic truths, the certainty *behind* firm
surfaces. Abrahams' defence of these truths is at the same time a
defence of the private realm. His defence is against the exigencies
of what, in an early poem, he describes as 'this climate of storms'.
Privacy is a hard-earned luxury (Abrahams is physically disabled).
Health and safety need to be won from the world. But this winning
is also a metaphor for the struggle to embody a liberal ethos that
became increasingly embattled with the radicalisation of the resis-
tance struggle. As he says in a more light hearted moment:

The individualist adult bourgeois,
wealthy in choices and secrets,
respectful of the neighbour's privacy
has had it.

Here we need to be careful: to talk of liberalism in South Africa is
not to refer to a single ideology, but to a set of cultural tendencies
some of which, in the context of political extremism, entailed a
number of common dilemmas, proceeding from the failure of
essentially liberal humanist principles to maintain any clear-cut
ethical coherence. Its condition is a state of tortured moral and
emotional conflict. *I deplore the state, but refuse to engage in, or
endorse those (non-peaceful) actions that would result in a juster*

society. I do not have the will or the ability to destroy the state, and therefore am forced helplessly to endure the times, while benefiting directly and indirectly from a system I hate. These are the kinds of impasses that the liberal has to negotiate. The engagement ultimately results in paralysis. In 'Spring report' nothing can be done except the opening of the gate for a dog. Equally it finds expression in a kind of knowing denial:

> Don't say it unless
> the night yields up your head
> or the broken sand sustains your foot.
> Don't say it unless you find
> music under the nails that scraped the door.
>
> ('Don't say it')

But if, from a distance, these poems therefore seem like inert objects (they have often been treated as straightforward statements of conviction), from close up they are a storm of colliding particles. There is hardly an Abrahams poem in which the images and ideas don't tussle with and contradict each other, or rebel against the harness into which the poet would set them. In 'Thresholds of tolerance', for instance, the poet would leave the revolutions of the street to those who have eyes and anger; but his description of the way he would hunt his private life, shows him to be just this kind of revolutionary: *he* is blessed with vision, *he* rages, his solitary pursuits are *literally* revolutionary: 'I turn inside my room/turn, turn'. In 'Winter report' a moment of solitary beauty – the poet's inhabiting of his private space (that most sacred realm of liberalism) – is more terrifying than uplifting. In this poem the position he favours is that of inner unity, what he eschews is confusion and defiance. But in 'To the idealistic killers', the revolutionary comrades whom he eschews for being 'strict kings of thought' are scorned precisely because of their unity of perception, while temptation and confusion are his preserve. Abrahams' poems never cease to engage in dialogue. There is not a bold truth stated, the fragility of which is not at some point conceded. His sensitivity to the imperilled status of the views he *nevertheless* holds, informs some of his most successful poems. Ultimately this 'nevertheless' sits at the centre of his complex of dilemmas out of which he writes. In the final account it makes his stance heroic.

In the polarised literary arena of the last three decades, the desire to inhabit the private life, and the will to identify, to engage political realities, to assert solidarities, were characteristically cast as contrary impulses, gestures of opposing cultural aesthetics. But even at the height of these debates poets were making nonsense of such terms, and no more so than in the very different oeuvres of Ingrid de Kok and Tatamkhulu Afrika.

Many of the voices in de Kok's earliest poems – 'At this resort', 'Leavetaking', 'My father would not show us' – speak out of overwhelming loss, resignation to loss, acceptance of the absence of love. The state of emotional exile is, in poems like 'This thing we learn from others', 'To drink its water', 'Shadows behind, before', a theme that de Kok, like Nortje before her, makes her own. But while Nortje achieved his finest poems largely through his inhabiting of the myth of exile, many of de Kok's poems explore too states of the most intimate kind of possession.

Identification in these poems is often an act of absorption, of physically bringing the world into the body. In 'To drink its water' the body is flooded with sense perception, as the sun's heat permeates the skin, as water enters the gut. Knowledge, too, in 'Shadows behind, before', is embodied in place. The world's entry into the body is also the body's entry into the world. With a dissolving of boundaries that is the premise on which de Kok's finest poems rest, the perceiving subject becomes part of an enclosed entity in intimate communication with itself. What takes place in the world at large, and the concerns of a private life are very often indistinguishable. What we bring to the world, and what the world brings to us, merge into each other, the origins of sensation levelled in the distillation into words.

In those poems that grow out of a sense of what it is to be in possession of, to be possessed by, a place, the external world becomes a subtle instrument of perception. Through landscape the deepest realities are sensed. The pressure of frictions, deep fissures, cool killings are, in 'Ground wave', communicated by wind, mountains, scorpions. This is not to say that the cool killings of 'Ground wave' are metaphors for political violence that takes place outside of the immediate world of the poem; rather they are expressions of a state of perception in which the world is sensed, literally constructed, given the fact of their occurrence. The questions we ask in engaging with these poems are *What made necessary the choice of this particular combination of observations? What has caused this surface to take on the precise appearance that it has?* Such poems are literally impressions, moulded shapes that express and capture within their forms an impression of the forces that create them, as a gust of wind might be caught in the wave of a frozen sea, or as the action of bubbling mud is preserved in the morphology of ancient rocks.

There are many South African poets who have been revolutionaries, many whose political activity informs their poetry. But few have written as directly out of the ordinary experience of the radicalised public – that collection of anonymous faces fleeting across the television screen – as Tatamkhulu Afrika. In lifting one 'I-experience' from that momentarily collective 'we', Afrika's poetry invests the faceless crowd with a humanity usually obscured. His poetry concretises what is often reduced to abstraction. It draws strength from the closeness it maintains to the event itself, from a sense of urgency and immediacy we associate more with reportage (so often do these poems have the stark, prosy feel of black and white documentary footage). Above all these poems draw strength from their unfailing commitment to the task of describing what it is like to *feel*.

Afrika writes out of his own life, and yet that perceiving 'I' – for all its sensitivities and idiosyncrasies – often implies a community brought together by shared experience. 'We drone', Afrika says – (that 'we' handled always with humility and care, claiming only the fact of a commonality of experience, not an exclusive authority to define it) –

> not with the fat,
> mellow hum of bees,
> but the thin
> snivelling of the fly;
> or we roar, faces turned
> to the never-listening sky,
> cacophonous as ass or mule

This poetry is made out of the experiences of people worn down by suffering to nothing more than themselves. His voice is that of the abused and defeated, those who became the medium through which the revolution took place, 'beaten till the dumb/tongue festers into sound'.

Afrika has associated himself with a genre of political poetry that achieved prominence in the 1980s, one of the functions of which was to serve as a 'weapon of the struggle'. 'Maqabane' is in many ways Afrika's equivalent of Livingstone's 'The waste land at Station 14', a defence here of the kind of poetry of which his work is a prominent achievement: the political poem, the poem that draws (some of) its strength from its engagement with the

political struggle, that in some sense wakes the sleeping heart and
steels the timid spine, which *stakes its success* on being able to do
this; and in doing so, makes art from the vocabulary of a partic-
ular political and social experience: the rally, the protesting crowd,
the toyi-toyi, the act of state terror, the act of defiance, the funeral,
the work-queue, the robbery, the sufferings of poverty, the
violence, fear, anomie, solidarity, desperation and triumph that
variously attend these experiences. 'Maqabane' not only asserts,
but enacts these strengths in a skilful denunciation of those who
would denounce the political:

> The familiar is suddenly behind.
> The grey men, the grey
> singers of irrelevant song,
> they who hid
> behind the stillness of their hands,
> slot into the patterns of our heels.

(That these grey singers are partly phantoms – one of a number of
stereotypes invented in a polarised literary community for the
purposes of mutual recrimination – is of secondary importance.)

Afrika is a 'political poet', one of those *hurt* into poetry. But as
in the case of all significant writers, of all the writers collected in
this anthology, any sobriquet demands immediate qualification.
In Tatamkhulu Afrika's poetry political themes merge seamlessly
with the social, personal and religious. These poems do not
embody a single defining *telos*. What they are about is co-
incidental with what they are: the creation of one who, to use
Jensma's phrase, has aspired to do no more than sense his situa-
tion; or to use Merleau-Ponty's, to create a poetry that embraces
its own origins.

Adam Schwartzman
Johannesburg, May 1999

Arthur Nortje

Waiting

The isolation of exile is a gutted
warehouse at the back of pleasure streets:
the waterfront of limbo stretches panoramically –
night the beautifier lets the lights
dance across the wharf.
I peer through the skull's black windows
wondering what can credibly save me.
The poem trails across the ruined wall
a solitary snail, or phosphorescently
swims into vision like a fish
through a hole in the mind's foundation, acute
as a glittering nerve.

Origins trouble the voyager much, those roots
that have sipped the waters of another continent.
Africa is gigantic, one cannot begin
to know even the strange behaviour furthest
south in my xenophobic department.
Come back, come back mayibuye
cried the breakers of stone and cried the crowds
cried Mr. Kumalo before the withering fire
mayibuye Afrika.

Now there is the loneliness of lost
beauties at Cabo de Esperancia, Table Mountain:
all the dead poets who sang of spring's
miraculous recrudescence in the sandscapes of Karoo
sang of thoughts that pierced like arrows, spoke
through the strangled throat of multi-humanity
bruised like a python in the maggot-fattening sun.

You with your face of pain, your touch of gaiety,
with eyes that could distil me any instant
have passed into some diary, some dead journal

now that the computer, the mechanical notion
obliterates sincerities.

The amplitude of sentiment has brought me no nearer
to anything affectionate,
new magnitude of thought has but betrayed
the lustre of your eyes.

You yourself have vacated the violent arena
for a northern life of semi-snow
under the Distant Early Warning System:
I suffer the radiation burns of silence.
it is not cosmic immensity or catastrophe
that terrifies me:
it is solitude that mutilates
the night bulb that reveals ash on my sleeve.

Immigrant

Don't travel beyond
Acton at noon in the intimate summer light
of England

to Tuskaloosa, Medicine Hat, preparing
for flight

dismissing the blond aura of the past
at Durban or Johannesburg
no more chewing roots or brewing riots

Bitter costs exorbitantly at London
airport in the neon heat
waiting for the gates to open

Big boy breaking out of the masturbatory
era goes
like eros over atlantis (sunk
in the time-repeating seas, admire our
tenacity)

jetting into the bulldozer civilization
of Fraser and Mackenzie
which is the furthest west that man has gone

A maple leaf is in my pocket.
X-rayed, doctored at Immigration
weighed in at the Embassy
measured as to passport, smallpox, visa
at last the efficient official informs me
I am an acceptable soldier of fortune, don't

tell the Commissioner
I have Oxford poetry in the satchel
propped between my army surplus boots
for as I consider Western Arrow's
pumpkin pancake buttered peas and chicken canadian style
in my mind's customs office
questions fester that turn the menu
into a visceral whirlpool. You can see
that sick bags are supplied.

Out portholes beyond the invisible propellers
snow mantles the ground peaks over Greenland.
What ice island of the heart has weaned
you away from the known white kingdom
first encountered at Giant's Castle?
You walked through the proteas nooked in the sun rocks
I approached you under the silver trees.
I was cauterized in the granite glare
on the slopes of Table Mountain, I was baffled
by the gold dumps of the vast Witwatersrand
when you dredged me from the sea like a recent fossil.

Where are the mineworkers, the compound Africans,
your Zulu ancestors, where are
the root-eating, bead-charmed Bushmen, the Hottentot sufferers?
Where are the governors and sailors of the
Dutch East India Company, where are
Eva and the women who laboured in the castle?
You are required as an explanation.

Glaciers sprawl in their jagged valleys,
cool in the heights, there are mountains and mountains.
My prairie beloved, you whose eyes are
less forgetful, whose fingers are less oblivious
must write out chits for the physiotherapy customers
must fill out forms for federal tax.

Consolatory, the air whiskies my veins.
The metal engines beetle on to further destinations.
Pilot's voice reports over Saskatchewan
the safety of this route, the use of exits,
facility of gas masks, Western Arrow's
miraculous record. The flat sea washes
in Vancouver bay. As we taxi in
I find I can read the road signs.

Maybe she is like you, maybe most women
deeply resemble you, all of them are
all things to all poets: the cigarette girl
in velvet with mink nipples, fishnet thighs,
whose womb is full of tobacco.
Have a B.C. apple in the A.D. city of the saviour,
and sing the centennial song.

Episodes with unusables

I

At dawn I rise to water.
Smelling the stucco and my shoes, leaning
into a wisp of air through shafted sunbeams:
it is another relief to be alone.

My liquid drops ammonia jewels
smoking in a net of grass.
Such a brief while the art of scintillation
lives in a miniature rainbow, the spring
earth tells me that all my words now,
my winter phrases, my wrought sentences
are dead as the thin conversation of evenings.

II

Tomatoes sprout in the garden, green
lettuce, the cool potatoes of the earth:
seeds we had thrown there, through the window,
through the door, where you
stood ready to make love, guarding my movements,
accepting my muscles, and I was thinking
how we were two, meshed in a kind of tenacity.

We have not watched
the sun shrivel the skin and eating
the juice of the unusable.
We have been locked in sleep, you have been fearing
the third growth, the fruit of nature.
I have groped in the rubbery darkness,
your cry has shattered all my integuments,
the total ecstasy has laid me waste.

I have loved you. We have not seen
the patience of waiting the seeds suffered,
the weathers they withstood in their infinite wisdom,
the tiny roots that felt their way into life,
the tendrils that clung.
Your hair fell over my eyes,
your aching beauty held me rooted.

Night ferry

Origins – they are dim in time, colossally
locked in the terrible mountain, buried in seaslime,
or vapourized, being volatile. What purpose
has the traveller now, whose connection is cut
with the whale, the wolf or the albatross? What does your small
                                        mouth
tell of supernovas or of chromosomes?
There are ivory graveyards in jungled valleys,
rainbow treasures, harps that sing in the wind,

fabled wrecks where the dead sailors sleep and a cuttlefish
sleeps on a bed of old doubloons.

                                                    Black bows
cleave water, suffer the waves. Finding the wet
deck, funnels, covered cargo, lifeboats
roped mute above the seasurge, pit-pat beats
the heart against the rail:
my flesh of salt clings to its molecules.

Oily and endless the stream is a truth drug. Pick
up signals from vast space, gather a ghoulish cry
from an astronaut lost for ever, his electronic
panels blipping with danger signs. Below
crushed like the foil on a Cracker Barrel cheese pack
a nuclear submarine no longer muscles
into the thunderous pressure. Is it the infinite
sound I hear that's going where? and to
whom can the intelligence be given? who are you?
Not only this, but also
between us the sensory network registers
potential tones, imaginable patterns
for there are destinies as well as destinations.

Screw churns through the superstructured
centuries of shut night, washing waters:
waves dip away, swell back, break open
in froth swaths and moon cobbles.
A snatch of Bach that intervenes
fluently pours through the portholes of my ears.
Boat on the Irish waters though I hear
poignant voices, whisper of snow, spring forests.
That set up plangencies, and issue oddthoughts.
With the ephemeral melody transistored.
Your eyes also seem to feature.

O are you daylight, love, to diminish my mist?
Siren, or the breeze's child, forgetful
while reaching through my bones?
In rest rooms people crowd, sleeping fug-
postured. Anyway of whom do I think?

I find an empty bunk, bend
under the muffled light, lie
in half-sleep, knock knock goes
the who's there night – a to-fro bottle tinkles.
It is the seasway, wavespeak, dance of angles.
Listen and you listen. Those are bilge-pipes.
Some are nightsounds, far from bird cries. Or a shark's snore.
The radius of consciousness is infinite, but seesaws.

Obscene are the unborn children, insane are the destitute
                                                    mothers,
I do not think, who have known them, disowned them.
The contours of cowdung, or snow in the cold hills
criss-crossing earthwards, or zigzag catgut
stitches on chest incisions – these are the merely
straightline rhythms, level planes, the simplicity ratio.
Then there's you
who must somewhere exist to be regarded
as needy, needed, night-bound: a cherished enigma.

Native's letter

Habitable planets are unknown or too
far away from us to be
of consequence. To be of
value to his homeland must the wanderer
not weep by northern waters, but love
his own bitter clay
roaming through the hard cities, tough
himself as coffin nails.

Harping on the nettles of his melancholy,
keening on the blue strings of the blood,
he will delve into mythologies perhaps
call up spirits through the night.

Or carry memories apocryphal
of Tshaka, Hendrik Witbooi, Adam Kok,
of the Xhosa nation's dream
as he moonlights in another country:

but he shall also have
cycles of history
outnumbering the guns of supremacy.

Now and wherever he arrives
extending feelers into foreign scenes
exploring times and lives,
equally may he stand and laugh,
explode with a paper bag of poems,
burst upon a million televisions
with a face as in a Karsh photograph,
slave voluntarily in some siberia
to earn the salt of victory.

Darksome, whoever dies
in the malaise of my dear land
remember me at swim,
the moving waters spilling through my eyes:
and let no amnesia
attack at fire hour:
for some of us must storm the castles
some define the happening.

Reflections in a passing mirror

In the deepsea reaches you can not
get near China or call Peru:
nothing except
remember Pericles, perhaps
view an albatross
sight a blue whale.

In the constipated crust of earth
you may with difficulty
dig up Etruscan artifacts, translate
the stones of ages past,
piece together with a scalpel
mammoth bones.

The ionosphere is riddled with
atoms of electric and a hairline
fracture can be fatal to
passengers of the sky.
You can not tell precisely when
the sun will blow its fuse.

Now beautiful is the love thing
sweet the word
peace to a thousand understandings:
the trumpeter swan in danger of extinction
is like the lizard of Komodo
saved, while our wars
go on.

In a discotheque
I feed on snacks, drinks
cacophony transmogrified to me
becomes a grotto silence, murk
this music, strobe greens, purples
and the spinning wheels of night, neoned outside
with the glare that flares between
the living and the dead.

Tearsweat, smoke, and sentiment,
blood coursing over drowned islands
where once the heart was beached.
Again I have not washed, I smell,
but why blush in the dark of life
when this booze breath is ripe
and words nullifying?
No sin against the world
can be committed by a heartbeat.

Because the brow burns
and the nostrils quiver
and the loins hunger or scream rape
sometimes
I never
forget in the middle
of nothing but a love ache every day
the gifted past, unspoilable.

Nasser is dead

Are not the Arabs cousins of the Jews?
Millions pour into Cairo
whose grief is inconsolable.
No-one
can stem the spread of fire of the flow of tears.

I think of the sons of Africa sometimes
and my heart bursts.
When I think of Chaka or Christ the rebel
my heart bursts.

The Queen of Sheba comes from the south.
Solomon, they say, was wise. David was strong, killed giants.
I have heard of Cleopatra proving
very wily, very
beautiful. And my heart bursts.

Hulks of ships clog Suez,
sandbagged bunkers on either side.
The Red Sea ports are closed.
Jordan cannot be crossed,
the Syrians are punished for their impunity.
Palestine with its ragged refugees
is won or lost, depending on who speaks the word
through the barrel of whose gun.
They are still fighting in Amman.
At the Wailing Wall they have stopped
knocking their heads against the stone, a
brief respite.

Farouk ails in Switzerland.
Is he not dead? I do not know.
So much has happened since the Ptolemies reigned
and the British marshals and generals withdrew.
One may say that Napoleon
departed in haste, there are readings and schools
of history, someone translated the Rosetta Stone-hieroglyphics,
and the Sahara is timeless.

So much water has drained from the heartland lakes
and yet they never dry up.
So much has happened between Khufu, between Cheops
and the liberation of the fellahin. All over Africa marched the
                                                    ravagers,
Alexandria burnt and flames ate the pages of books.

But are not the Arabs cousins of the Jews?
Aswan, that great work,
was almost broken by the raiders.
Abu Simbel was first saved piece by piece: I understand
it cost the Americans millions.

One wonders who
plundered the Pyramids, found the tunnels.
No worse than a bank
robbery, stealing the mummies.

Some of the monstrous blocks have fallen
claimed by the desert.
And all over Africa the gourds are broken,
the calabashes empty at one time or another.
Spears are buried or removed
but don't we all eat with knives?
We cannot be converted in a decade.
Boots litter Gaza. The carnage ebbs and flows.
Rusting tanks are the last monuments.
Millions mourn a train longer than the Nile:
their flood of tears cannot be beaten back,
and the rich silt is the salt on women's cheeks,
sweat on the brows of men.

Sonnet one

Supremely individual, flamboyant, proud,
insane and thirsty for a stable life,
attacked by love's dementia, and predicaments and loud
laughter at the skyjackings, world troubles and world strife,

in cosmopolitan dives of some metropolis
I know that this is not the universe,
and how the rain shines through the sun and stars
explode within a galaxy remains mysterious.

The poisoned spring has bubbled through my veins:
Young Venus lay in rags I loved her so –
Dog of ferocity. The golden road turned blue
becomes a damp and rampant thoroughfare for sins
of carnality, of turpitude. The smelly and the raw
crowds that disgust me are also those I adore.

Sonnet two

I have drunk up nights and spent the days
in wild pursuits, life of the libertine:
do not repent, confess, seek remedies.
The bourgeois sinners are banned from where I've been.

The desperate either go mad with self-disgust
or steal or rob from the immaculate:
through sheer loathing some have stood and passed
water against the walls. Expectorate

politely into your chamber pots. I speak
to you for whom spittoons are made, who buy
furbelows and leopard skins, antiques.
Will you not read it, this my poetry,
calling it uncouth: it makes you sick?
You serve your tea in china that's authentic.

All hungers pass away

All hungers pass away,
we lose track of their dates:
desires arise like births,
reign for a time like potentates.

I lie and listen to the rain
hours before full dawn brings
forward a further day and winter sun
here in a land where rhythm fails.

Wanly I shake off sleep,
stare in the mirror with dream-puffed eyes:
I drag my shrunken corpulence
among the tables of rich libraries.

Fat hardened in the mouth,
famous viands tasted like ash:
the mornings-after of a sweet escape
ended over bangers and mash.

I gave those pleasures up,
the sherry circuit, arms of a bland girl
Drakensberg lies swathed in gloom,
starvation stalks the farms of the Transvaal.

What consolation comes
drops away in bitterness.
Blithe footfalls pass my door
as I recover from the wasted years.

The rain abates. Face-down
I lie, thin arms folded, half-aware
of skin that tightens over pelvis.
Pathetic, this, the dark posture.

Soliloquy: South Africa

It seems me speaking all the lonely time,
whether of weather or death in winter,
or, as you expected and your eyes asked, love,
even to the gate where goodbye could flame it.
The last words that issue from the road
are next day regretted because meant so much.

All one attempts is talk in the absence
of others who spoke and vanished
without so much as an echo.
I have seen men with haunting voices
turned into ghosts by a piece of white paper
as if their eloquence had been black magic.

Because I have wanted so much, your you,
I have waited hours and tomorrows, dogged
and sometimes doggish but you often listened.
Something speaks on when something listens:
in a room a fly can be conversation,
or a moth which challenges light but suffers.

Should you break my heart open, revive the muscle
for March grows on with mounting horror:
how to be safe is our main worry.
To keep you happy I shall speak more,
though only in whispers of freedom
now that desire has become subversive.

The gulls are screaming. I speak out to sea.
Waters, reared for attack, break forward:
without a word, this violence. From the cliffs
above the warm, shark-breeding sea that drowns
the oracle of the vibrant air I walk
and hear the ropes that thrash against the flagpoles.

The wind's voice moans among willows.
Would you say that air can move so much?
It echoes so much of ourselves. In you
lies so much speech of mine buried
that for memory to be painless I must knife it.
it seems me speaking all the lonely time.

Cape Town, 1963

Hangover

Dissatisfaction invites me nowhere
for even profit and loss discussion:
silence keeps me home, I'm lonely.
Lately escape became the fashion.

I am alone here now, here living
with shoals of fragments, a voice hoarse like rubble
shifted by currents.

'Bill is in for an infinite while
and that's why Tom went underground.'
But this is confidential
(better stick that poem away
before the Special boys raise hell).

After the pub, after blur in the vague room
wine carries me to sleep.
Groaning awake I ask for time and water.
Snores answer me and rats
clawing wallpapers with tiger paws.
No lice, luckily I'm a bastard.

What I possess is oddments mostly
picked up in O.K. Bazaars at cost price
(there I saw rich people hunt in the basement
or perhaps they were hiding).

My face in the basin after
gulping a goblet of aspirin
scared the mirror with subtle laughter
(I remember these bits and pieces blindly).
That day in a bungalow revolving events
through love and liquor
before your banning.
Supper at the Naaz, instant
coffee at nine, coming home tomorrow.

Raymond's Tretchikoff smashed from the bare wall
when Frenchie demonstrated football;
shebeens all shuttered made it worse,
Tom Dooley sleeping on his purse.

Turned into shadows and echoes, those whispers.
The sun has gone under the sunset,
the moon squats with a lonely pallor.

In case of foul play, imprisonment, death
by drinking (identity is
268430: KLEURLING
Pretoria register, male 1960)
inform Mrs Halford, Kromboom Road, Crawford,
house without garden. No reward.

October 1963

At Lansdowne Bridge

After the whoosh of doors slid shut
at Lansdowne Bridge I swim in echoes.
Who fouled the wall O people?
FREE THE DETAINEES someone wrote there.

Black letters large as life stare you
hard by day in the black face;
above the kikuye grass to the sandflats
goes the boorish clang-clang of railways.

Darkness neutralizes the request
till dawn falls golden and sweet,
though a sudden truck by night
cornering, holds it in spidery light.

Cape Town, May 1964

Your absence

The moon be thanked for what
last night's surrender released
within her clasping limbs.
Numb in a morning body my bleak
find is a weary drizzle.
Life's ache throbs up from zero.

I flatter a casual
acquaintance sometimes.
Or entertain nubile
strangers completely
alone in this same

house where now pan's oil
ambushes albumen,
water strikes
icy aluminium.
The yolk quivers,
the leak's irreparable.

You would have opened
windows, touched
steamed mirrors.
Stood pensively musing
how many Rothmans and Stuyvesant stubs
it would take to fill one silver ashtray.

Sublunary illusion lacking
I slurp coffee
very realistically. Summer means
that days are long and in your absence searing.

1965

Mongane Wally Serote

Hell, well, heaven

I do not know where I have been,
But Brother,
I know I'm coming.
I do not know where I have been,
But Brother,
I know I heard the call.
Hell! where I was I cried silently
Yet I sat there until now.
I do not know where I have been,
But Brother,
I know I'm coming:
I come like a tide of water now,
But Oh! There's sand beneath me!
I do not know where I have been
To feel so weak, Heavens! so weary.
But Brother,
Was that Mankunku's horn?
Hell! my soul aches like a body that has been beaten,
Yet I endured till now.
I do not know where I have been,
But Brother,
I know I'm coming.
I do not know where I have been
To have fear so strong like the whirlwind (will it be that brief?)
But Brother,
I know I'm coming.
I do not know where I have been,
But Brother,
Was that Dumile's figure?
Hell, my mind throbs like a heart beat, there's no peace;
And by body of wounds – when will they be scars? –
Yet I can still walk and work and still smile.
I do not know where I have been
But Brother,

I know I'm coming.
I do not know where I have been,
But Brother,
I have a voice like the lightning-thunder over the mountains.
But Oh! there are copper lightning conductors for me!
I do not know where I have been
To have despair so deep and deep and deep
But Brother,
I know I'm coming.
I do not know where I have been
But Brother,
Was that Thoko's voice?
Hell, well, Heavens!

from *No Baby Must Weep*

1

i am the man you will never defeat
i will be the one to plague you
your children are cursed
if you walk this earth, where i too walk
and you tear my clothes and reach for my flesh
and tear my flesh to reach my blood
and you spill my blood to reach my bones
and you smash my bones and hope for my soul
the wind and the mountains and the stars
the sun the moon
saw you
i am the man you will never defeat
my song will merge with the breeze
my tears will freeze in time
you will walk the earth whose dust is my bones
and the sun will set like my eyes when they close for
the last time
and the moon will shine on my scream
i
i am the man you will never defeat
when the trees rattle you shall hear my last footsteps
this won't be your world

i am the man you will never defeat
i will be your shadow, to be with you always
and one day
when the sun rises
the shadows will move, heaving like a tired chest
there shall be millions of shadows
heaving
and the earth shall be cold
and the river will freeze
and the plants will refuse to grow
and the earth shall be dark
and the river shall be dark
and we will be alone

no man can defeat another man
we can sing together
make each other together
we can eat together
make the world together

no man can defeat another man

*

2

i
i look at your face my mama
it's a long long time since i sat on your lap
felt the warmth of your breath as you tried to kiss me
as you teased me
as your bosom heaved with the love for your little boy
it's a long long time ago since i sat on your back
listened to the noise of your feet as they sang
a rhythm with the earth
and the song sang in my bowels
it's a long long time
i
i have heard your voice pierce the passage of my secrets
as i groped in the dark street
searching for me

in broken automobiles
growing
behind the toilet which dripped its pus and spilled it in
the air
running
from your long long voice which always held me by the scruff
teaching me shame
it's a long long time ago mama
when your eye with its fierce light pinned me against the wall
and my little heart searched my little head
and i could only turn out a little scream
and the little hoofs in my chest made me want to lie down
and rest

mama
hold this my hand which you made with your blood and your
flesh
i am weary from running now
this earth ate my heels
the breeze has bruised my face
the sun has burnt my flesh
my shoulders are tired
you never told me this could happen mama
yet i know you love me
i know you love
i
i have seen your eyes wink, wink wink
and have felt your gentle hands search for my peace
in this the dark hour of my time
for my life
for this little droplet of your blood
i have seen your eyes wink
wink
giving birth to blind shadows cold shadows
when your sight seized me so gently like a cat
would bite its kittens
from the many blind footsteps to the soft mat
let me drink your love mama
let it spill its warmth on my cold bosom
so when the sun bursts into flames
and the moon comes tumbling down
and the stars shut their twinkle

i
i can remember the warmth of your love
let me into your rhythmic gait which bore insults
let me into your beat of your heart where love overflows
let me touch the robe of your flesh
i can hear the one-time man tear the horizon with his scream
and the vast sky is looking at me
i can touch the fear of the children which drops out of
their eyes
and the huge many trees shake their heads,
mama
let me into your bursting passion
soothe my wound let me love
oh you black mother
black woman
mama
your smile that paves through the wounds and the hurt
breaks me
like a twig loaded with green leaves and ripe fruit
mama
let me fall to the earth let me fall to this soil
let my rest be a seed
if i will take this fall
gently, gently
with my bare feet and my naked body
with my red heart and unfathom the depths of my soul
to the sky
the sun
the stars and the moon
to the mountains
the trees
if i will take this fall gently
gently
with my red heart and unfathom the depths of my soul
to this the earth
my mama
and with my clean fingers touch, just touch this deep love

*

3

i can say
here
the water spreads and spreads and spreads
and the banks of this earth
crack
like a door giving in to an angry man
i can say

those who cried and died whose graves sank
went below the water
i can say
the water is dark
the water is deep
the water spreads and spreads and spreads
i can say
the water is wide
the water is dark
the water is deep
i can say
ah the silent saints, the unforgiving saints
i can say
the littered tissue papers
trailing me up to here where i come, i stop
the soiled rainbow-coloured tissue papers
trailing me up to here where i come, i stop
the soiled rainbow-coloured tissue papers
filled with tears
pus
sweat
i can say
these streets this town this land grows big kaffirs indeed
i can say
we sang
and smiled
and clapped hands
while the wind whipped our ears
while we crowded the back of the truck like animals
i can say
we watched and talked and laughed about your clean faces
i can say

while sorrow
and the pain of my wounded heart made my one-time childlike
                                                    face debris

yet i smiled
the stars the moon the sky sighed because they couldn't comfort
                                                    me

i can say hallelujah
and clap my hands
and do my dance
and ring my laughter into the air like birds do their whistles
i can say
and i not the one who recalls footsteps, hasty, running
on the thick dusty shadows of the night
shadows carrying a frightened little heart on their palms
a red heart
shot in the night in the street for stealing a car
shit like that
getting my children killed
i can say
hurrah
i can hear voices and voices and voices
saying child
honey-child
i love you
i can hear voices and voices and voices replying hurrah
and the footsteps have died now
here we are
here we come
one man a million men
come stop here
where the footsteps freeze beneath the heels
on this sand
spreading and spreading they say earth becomes earth
here we are now
who will listen
the water is dark
the water is deep
and the water spreads and spreads
and the moon must tumble down...
let me seep into africa
let this water
this sea

seep into me own me
and break my face into its moods
break my chest
break my heart into its fathoms where no hands reach
let the salt of this sea
settle down like a dove come home, into the wounds that
this earth made in my bosom
ah
let this water, this sea
these waves
these colours
this movement
this wide deep blue solid reality break me down like it has rocks

africa
where humility seeps into rocks and roots
singing the heart-breaking tune
africa
harness your cow...

what is the matter, nothing matters any more
my brother died
folded like a paper wrung by angry hands
and last night a baby came and departed into death
smooth
like a man walking into a door
ah
what's the matter
to belong, to be owned, to be locked
in a million eyes
this water
the river the sea
dark
deep
smashing and whistling above the air
choking the bird's whistle

ah
nothing matters any more
nothing

my gait was beaten until it broke like a twig
and it is i who heard the laughter
while i choked my cry
i could look into no face they were all bright like the sun
the bone of my heart broke
and the marrow spilled

ah nothing matters any more
nothing

i can say
i
i have gone beyond the flood now
i left the word on the flood
it echoes
in the depth the width
i am beyond the flood

i can say
these eyes
this water this river this flood
washed me
i can say
one day the word will break

i can say
one day the laughter will break

i can say
one day the sky will weep
i can say one day
this flower
will stand in the bright bright sun
this flower will have no petals
one day

ah
africa
is this not your child come home

Ofay-watcher looks back

I want to look at what happened;
That done,
As silent as the roots of plants pierce the soil
I look at what happened,
Whether above the houses there is always either smoke or dust,
As there are always flies above a dead dog.
I want to look at what happened.
That done,
As silent plants show colour: green,
I look at what happened,
When houses make me ask: do people live there?
As there is something wrong when I ask – is that man alive?
I want to look at what happened,
That done,
As silent as the life of a plant that makes you see it
I look at what happened
When knives creep in and out of people
As day and night into time.
I want to look at what happened,
That done,
As silent as plants bloom and the eye tells you: something has
                                                    happened.

I look at what happened
When jails are becoming necessary homes for people
Like death comes out of disease,

I want to look at what happened.

City Johannesburg

This way I salute you:
My hand pulses to my back trousers pocket
Or into my inner jacket pocket
For my pass, my life,
Jo'burg City.
My hand like a starved snake rears my pockets
For my thin, ever lean wallet,
While my stomach groans a friendly smile to hunger,

Jo'burg City.
My stomach also devours coppers and papers
Don't you know?
Jo'burg City, I salute you;
When I run out, or roar in a bus to you,
I leave behind me, my love,
My comic houses and people, my dongas and my ever
                                        whirling dust,
My death
That's so related to me as a wink to the eye.
Jo'burg City
I travel on your black and white and robotted roads
Through your thick iron breath that you inhale
At six in the morning and exhale from five noon.
Jo'burg City
That is the time when I leave you,
When your neon flowers flaunt from your electrical wind,
That is the time when I leave you,
When your neon flowers flaunt their way through the
                                        falling darkness
On your cement trees.
And as I go back, to my love,
My dongas, my dust, my people, my death,
Where death lurks in the dark like a blade in the flesh,
I can feel your roots, anchoring your might, my feebleness
In my flesh, in my mind, in my blood,
And everything about you says it,
That, that is all you need of me.
Jo'burg City, Johannesburg,
Listen when I tell you,
There is no fun, nothing, in it,
When you leave the women and men with such frozen
                                        expressions,
Expressions that have tears like furrows of soil erosion,
Jo'burg City, you are dry like death,
Jo'burg City, Johannesburg, Jo'burg City.

Alexandra

Were it possible to say,
Mother, I have seen more beautiful mothers,
A most loving mother,
And tell her there I will go,
Alexandra, I would have long gone from you.

But we have only one mother, none can replace,
Just as we have no choice to be born,
We can't choose mothers;
We fall out of them like we fall out of life to death.

And Alexandra,
My beginnings are knotted to you,
Just like you knot my destiny.
You throb in my inside silences
You are silent in my heart-beat that's loud to me.
Alexandra often I've cried.
When I was thirsty my tongue tasted dust,
Dust burdening your nipples.
I cry Alexandra when I am thirsty.
Your breasts ooze the dirty waters of your dongas,
Waters diluted with the blood of my brothers, your children,
Who once chose dongas for death-beds.
Do you love me Alexandra, or what are you doing to me?

You frighten me, Mama,
You wear expressions like you would be nasty to me,
You frighten me, Mama,
When I lie on your breast to rest, something tells me
You are bloody cruel.
Alexandra, hell
What have you done to me?
I have seen people but I feel like I'm not one,
Alexandra what are you doing to me?

I feel I have sunk to such meekness!
I lie flat while others walk on me to far places.
I have gone from you, many times,
I come back.
Alexandra, I love you;
I know
When all these worlds became funny to me
I silently waded back to you
And amid the rubble I lay,
Simple and black.

Her name is 'Dooti'

Cutting off all to her thoughts,
Like a devoted florist his rose-branches before spring,
Dooti is a girl with a great future;
She has the world's greatest keys
In those excursions of the heart,
Or wherever it is we hold these keys;
Hullo–Goodbye;
Between that stands her name and needs,
And her face; silent.
We of the world have grown tired of listening
To names and needs;
We have closed curtains lately
To the future.
And everytime the truth peeps out at an awkward time,
For that is what the truth can do,
Our curtains become showy,
Like spoilt children among guests;
And our faces show
For there's nothing to beat faces –
They define;
Dooti's face shouts all that we won't bear,
We won't hear.
Her name is Dooti,
Her face knows her needs well,
And she's got the keys;
Hullo–Goodbye.

The three mothers

Yes;
This is the silence of our speedy uncurling youth-tangles
Forms folds, curves little surprised faces
That gape at our heritage,
Our age,
That grab son from mother like the cross did Jesus from Maria,
The faces that have eyes that are tears,
Tears from mothers,
Lord,
This has left me so silent!
Elizabeth comes in, food in hand, to feed us,
I can see her sadness. I can see her deep wish.
My heart mouths her misery. I'm silent. My friend is silent.
Hilda with her urges, her intuition dipping its tongue
Into the depths of our bitterness
She urges us on! On! not to fall.
And we watch, the little kingdoms, castles, of our mothers.

Tomorrow we know,
We shall be homeless, just that;
What a hunger!
Alina, my silence is that question
No son hates his mother be sure;
But love can wound.

Night-time

trees seem to sweat in the dark
and the street lights look like wet eyes
as the glow from the windows fades heavily on the drawn curtains
houses put their loaded shadows gently on the black earth,
hugh masekela sings
and roberta flak
percy sledge –
hooters break the singing of crickets like glass
and pierce the muted voices of talking homes
one car at the time, roars past,
a scooter,
hasty footsteps come and fade

soon people will sleep.
tomorrow the streets will groan with loads of footsteps,
hasty footsteps
running footsteps
hurrying to play hide and seek with dignity in the city,
inside the skyscrapers, where a breath is held.

Introit

I have lain on my back
flat like a long dead reptile
I lie here while my load clutches my heart like a frightened child
And the horrors of my stomach throb to my eyes
I am a black manchild
I am he who has defeated defeat
I am a surprise which surprises me
The load of the day leaves my shoulders red and bruised
But alas
the Chest of the night heaves into my eyes
The whores' scream and the barking dogs are my companions
The snap of life and the making of death have woven my strides
My thick footsteps pulsate on black shadows
They rumble, rumble like a journey with a destination
Aaahw the blackmanchild

I have lain on my back dead just like pulled out weeds
while blood flowed in me like a river
My pores have been holes pouring out sweat which flooded lies
I have built the day like every man has
I have broken the day to shadows which came and lay
                              gently over my house
I am no big blackman
I am a blackmanchild

I have tamed the stallion-woman beneath me
I have held children's hands in mine and led them
Alas the children
They have looked up at me as if my eyes were ripe fruit
                              dangling from a tree
the children have seen the sun shine into my eyes

they have seen my face glow silver with the light of the moon
maybe they have heard me weep too
for I have wept

The long road

we cannot lie on our back
we cannot stretch our legs and our arms
we cannot show our soft-white belly to the red hot sun
we cannot lie on our back
how, we ask –
is a long road measured?
does the marrow of the rock say
does the soil, pierced by the blade of the plough say
as it peels and rolls
as it tears
as it ripens into a wound that must receive a seed
does it say anything
with its agreeable whispers
as the blade cuts, and as it turns and rolls
the distance that measures the ability to wait –
for the seed
does the soil say anything?

the sun sings with heat here
we cannot show our soft-white belly to the sun
the sun has teeth

how is a long road measured

when the seasons
like a woman in love ask
through their eyes and face
through the tips of their fingers
as soft as a day old baby's flesh – they ask:
if love is so bare, what care do you have?

the seasons are strong
they mount time
they mount tops of trees
the seasons mount the sun and the moon
and ask

how is a long road measured?
the rumble of cattle hooves flow to the river
the river floods and flows
plants whistle through the soil

a man bare feet
red soiled clothes
and a heart, harder than a rail track
reads the sun and the river
and picks up a gun.

how, how is a long road measured?

if like the seasons
you have come and left
and come again

how is a long road measured

if the scars of your body
like soil receives the plough blade every season
begin to itch with expectation

how we ask, is a long road measured?

we will not lie on our back
and like a seedling of an aloe
solomon emerges
with thorns as bright as the sun rays,
the silence here is very familiar now.

mini
mkaba
molefe
paul peterson
we ask luthuli
mandela tambo
how is a long road measured?
when sticks of arrows thinner than a child's arm
now bloom like flowers in spring
bursting into red, blue, purple, orange flames
at sasol

how is a long road measured, we ask?

if you see my eyes
on my round face as if they were two naked breasts
and they stare and stare and stare
if you hear this silence
like a sigh of secret lovers in the dark
not wailing like breaking glass
and you see
a myriad of red, blue, green and yellow flames
scream to the silent sky
and when you touch –
as if a snake twirled and disturbed,
everything shifts and shifts
ah my beloved
this means time is here
when the little ones, like a seed
must pierce the ground, and let the winters pass by.

remember
those days when we sat around a brazaire
not far from us, the wind whistling and whistling
and we watched
the gait of the old
as they came back from work to die
or went to work to destroy their strength for nothing
remember how we did not understand
that they were carrying oppression on their shoulders
silent
and plotting?

today in
orlando
moroka
boysens
soekmekaar
dube
sasol
durban power station
new canada
red, blue, green and yellow flames scream to the silent sky.

Mafika Gwala

Beyond fences

A number in the boxhouse registry
They don't have to know you
They'll search for you in the dark
Should you look grey in that dark
They'll smear red paint over you
Should you remain black and red
They will call before dawn
– hoping to find you napping
Should they strike a miss
They'll pin you to the 'Wanted' list
Should they not find you next day
They'll be quick to say:
The communists have gone underground.

The amaPhephetha of Ophisweni
and the sons and nephews of Mazhiya
will sure bear me out
For all the tears from the mothers
of young braves at Isandlwana
Let me drink from the khamba of the elders
let me blow my nose into kraalmis
Let me seek through Life
    the sons and daughters of yesterday
The waters of the Inyalazi
have crocodiled me to Umthunzini
Where men received the drilled patience
of a root doctor
When shall I inhale once more the gardenia fragrance
of the Umngeni Valley in mid-Spring?

Let me take the lithe of the tiger
Let me steal the speed of the cheetah
let me track the paths
    of my hunting forefathers

Let me cut the riverpool
    with the sharp circle of the fish
Let me clutch with the wet grip
    of an eel
Let me cheat the wind
    with the hiss of the black mamba
Let me go the way of the elephant –
    and trumpet the past into the future
Let me wander in open veld
Let me wander amongst the trees
Let me wander in the bushes
Let me wander in the river valleys
Where the wind sings
Where the bird chirps melody
Where the flower smiles
Where the leaf in rustle blushes
Where the river guffaws
Where the rock browses.

Bonk'abajahile

And you once asked why
blacks
    lived so fast
    love so fast
    drink so fast
      die so fast
It doesn't start with eMalangeni;
It doesn't.
It starts with the number
you found smeared on the door
        of your home

– and you from school
– or from work.

      one and two
      three and four
      bonk'abajahile

The cement smile
of the teller at the bank
adopted as symbol of courtesy:
            'work and save
            wear smart
            get yourself a hi-fi/tv
            buy yourself a car!'

            one and two
            three and four
            bonk'abajahile

At Webber's I saw him
running like mad
on a futile marathon
after he'd grabbed a bag
from that farmer
who pronounced 'Mophela'
like 'amaphela'

I saw her pulling up her pantihose
fixing her semi-Afrowig
With a blue eye and spitting blood
after a fight with another
of Playboy Joe's girls;
Playboy Joe was already at Umgababa
pulling dagga zol with other majitas,
And at Umgababa Alice's Juba
wasn't sour this afternoon.
            one and two
            three and four
            bonk'abajahile

I saw him wave an Okapi
under the Umnqadodo Bridge
to settle scores born of a factory life;
Umgababa's guava tree broke
The guava fruit projectiled
onto Duma's car:
            Hammarsdale 1972.
The knife wound gave the telling of his death.
They covered his body with a Spinlon dustcoat

Waiting for someone to ring Inchanga 41.

> one and two
> three and four
> bonk'abajahile

Langashona's hand against his face
A face long dead to wind the story;
A flower plucked off in bud
Down UNIT ONE SOUTH.
Msingi's expressionless face
A face not squealing.
Bongi Ndlovu
She tried to run, to flee, to plead;
Whick! Whack!
Into flesh came the bushknife
On the sand dunes she collapsed
Waiting for fate to say it's over;
How she let her soul go
is a mystery to bemoan;
Can we blame her kind of life?
Can we blame the rage that held him
in spell?
If we are not saints
They'll try to make us devils;
If we refuse to be devils
They'll want to turn us into robots.
When criminal investigators
are becoming salesmen
When saints are ceasing to be saints
When devils are running back to Hell
It's the Moment of Rise or Crawl
When this place becomes Mpumalanga
With the sun refusing to rise
When we fear our blackness
When we shun our anger
When we hate our virtues
When we don't trust our smiles

> one and two
> three and four
> bonk'abajahile

Sing, how can we sing
  with chainblocks barring us
   the Malombo Sound?
Play, how can we play
  with games turning into nightmares?
Talk, should we not talk with deep
       open voices?
Wait, should we wait till the cows
       come home?

One small boy longs for summer

(for Bill Naughton)

The kettle hisses
Mother moves about the kitchen
sliding from corner to corner.
The fire from the stove
pierces into the marrow.
And mother pushing towards the stove
warns of the steam.
My young brother, Thamu, jerks my arm
violently: Stop leaning on me, your elbow
has sunk into my thigh.
   Apology
     I wasn't aware.

The kettle sings
   Some distant far-away song?
Mother picks it up
with an almost tender care.
Sets me thinking of a war-picture
The actor carefully setting the charge
and smiling all the time
   I'll also be a soldier
when I'm old – why, Uncle Shoba was one.
Father drops the paper on the table
he comes to join us
   – staring coldly round.
It's no frown really,

But he's grinding his jaws.
         Maybe it's the July
Handicap.

The kettle purrs now
Steam is escaping; it kisses the ceiling
and vanishes. Mother is pouring the violent waters
into the coffee-jug. Coffee.
Yes, I need some coffee – a mug of hot coffee.
Very rousing.
We can't play outside – I must not go, I know
         How we danced in the rain. We are so tired
of the winter: It's so dingy outside
We can't play inside – I'm so tied up.
It's so boring, I feel like bursting into
a cracking laughter; but father,
he'll go mad.
It's so steamy inside.
I feel I could bite the walls down.
If only it makes the winter pass.

An attempt at communication

Speak easy, brother
         There's a lively chick
         with a dainty smile.
         There's auntie's cool mama-look
         lest we start some shindig.
         The spark tells me
         I'm not all screwed, yes
         I'm booze-feeding, just.

Hot it cool, right
         We have the music-blues
         to bury the dead blue
         in us.
         Give yourself a forwardpush
         Africa rhythm –
         Start off and go.
         Then you're jazzhappy.

Cool it hot, yes
    That mbaqanga
    stirs you too?
    I can do my own
    Rock, Twist, and Jive.
    For I also have
    my muscles to loosen
    and to cringe.

    When it befits me.

Election pincers

The paper before him.
Badly weighing its paperless weight – and with peasant
caginess he dived into the pool of questions:
'You say the present policy has been good?'
'No, I did not say that. I merely asked you to choose,' said
the interpreter; shoulders levelled and his twitching nose
savouring a bored, tight understanding. He borrowed effort
to explain: 'For the ruling party you can always be sure of a
job; your child is assured a better education; and you, you
CAN retire to an old-age home in the greencountry
atmosphere of the Transkei.'

The old man balanced the points-cross and tick.
Then brushing his patched trousers: 'Does it mean FREE
SCHOOLING for my son? Will my wife not write letters for
clinic fees? And my cattle, won't they be culled?'

'Khehla, we don't own the day.'
'Son if I didn't know, I wouldn't have come so early.' –
Rounds of ammunition. Ready, fire!
'I have explained everything you have to know about the
whole thing. Now, are you not prepared to cast your vote?'
Rabid impatience – the white officer adjusts his Sunday tie,
a one-inch, thin stripes. Red and Black. Scorching glances.

'The other candidate – does he offer: higher wages, reduced
taxes, and more grazing land?'
Rugged silence. Pincered doubt.
The old man crossed beside favoured candidate. Then with
fingers provoking made another cross beside the opposing
candidate. He pushed the paper at the interpreter with gauged
expectancy. The interpreter frowned. Piggishly.
'Spoilt Vote.'

The jive

Mahlathini blues
plus Bra Thekwane's Movers
on a Tau Special
we jive through our problems
all that is left
of the black miseries jive
Mandela off'd to Robben Island
Boy Faraday off'd to Heaven or Hell
i don't know where
i'm only dead certain
of six feet underground
the ja-baas jive scares cowards
with Frankenstein monstereyes
and the jive continues
but we blacks got the wizard in us
we have the best soccer rocker in
Pele our mojo does us wonders
since we rock our church services
    we rock the Ninth Symphony too
    we rock our boxing
    we rock our maidens
just as sure
    we rock the whiteboat too
so's there'll be new Black folks coming
stepping it right on
for the end of the jive
we home in on Havanna rock
we home in on Miriam Makeba blues
and when the blues is gone
it will be long gone over
with the jive

Gumba, gumba, gumba

Been watching this jive
For too long.
That's struggle.
West Street ain't the place
To hang around any more;
Pavid's Building is gone.
Gone is Osmond's Bottle Store.
And West Street is like dry;
The dry of patent leather
When the guests have left.
And the cats have to roll like
Dice into the passageways...
Seeking a fix
While they keep off the jinx.
That's struggle.

Miasmic haze at 12 noon
Stretching into the wilderness
Of uniformed gables...
Vast and penetrating
As the Devil's eye.
At night you see another dream
White and monstrous;
Dropping from earth's heaven,
Whitewashing your own Black dream.
That's struggle.
Get up to listen
To Black screams outside;
With deep cries, bitter cries.
That's struggle.

Struggle is when
You have to lower your eyes
And steer time
With your bent voice.
When you drag along –
Mechanically.
Your shoulders refusing;
Refusing like a young bull
Not wanting to dive

Into the dipping tank
Struggle is keying your tune
To harmonize with your inside.

Witness a dachshund bitch shitting
A beautiful Black woman's figure too close by,
Her hand holding the strap;
In a whitelonely suburb.
Tramp the city
Even if you're sleepweary;
'Cos your Black arse
Can't rest on a 'Whites Only' seat.
Jerk your talk
Frown in your laughs
Smile when you ain't happy.
That's struggle.
Struggle is being offered choices that fink your smiles.
Choices that dampen your frown.
Struggle is knowing
What's lacking in your desires
'Cos even your desires are made
To be too hard for you to grab.

Seeing how far
You are from the abyss
Far the way your people are.
Searching your way out
Searching to find it;
Ain't nobody to cry for you.
When you know what's bugging your mama
Your mama coming from the white madam's.
When all the buses
Don't pick you up
In the morning, on your way to work.
'Cos there ain't even room to stand.
Maybe you squeezed all of Soweto,
Umlazi, Kwa-Mashu
Into one stretch of a dream;
Maybe Chatsworth, maybe Bonteheuwel.
Then you chased it & went after it;
It, the IT and ITS.
Perhaps you broke free.

If you have seen:
Seen queues at the off-course tote;
Seen a man's guts – the man walking still
Seen a man blue-eye his wife;
Seen a woman being kicked by a cop.

You seen struggle.
If you have heard:
Heard a man bugger a woman, old as his mother:
Heard a child giggle at obscene jokes
Heard a mother weep over a dead son;
Heard a foreman say 'boy' to a labouring oupa
Heard a bellowing, drunken voice in an alley.
You heard struggle.
Knowing words don't kill
But a gun does.
That's struggle.
For no more jive
Evening's eight
Ain't never late.
Black is struggle.

The children of Nonti

Nonti Nzimande died long, long ago
Yet his children still live.
Generation after generation, they live on;
Death comes to the children of Nonti
And the children of Nonti cry but won't panic
And there is survival in the children of Nonti.

Poverty swoops its deathly wings. But tough,
strong and witty are the children of Nonti.
The wet rains fall. The roads become like
the marshed rice paddies of the Far East;
And on these desolate roads there is song
Song in the Black voices of the children of Nonti.

Someone marries
The bride does not hide her face under the veil;
The maidens dance near the kraal
Dance before the 'make it merry' eyes
of the elders. The elders joshing it
on their young days.
There is still free laughter
in the children of Nonti.

An ox drops to the earth, then another;
Knives run into the meat. Making the feast
to be bloodfilled with Life.
The old, the dead, are brought into the Present
of continuous nature in the children of Nonti
Got to be a respecting with the children of Nonti.

When a daughter has brought shame
The woman show anger; not wrath.
And the illegitimate born is one of
the family.
When a son is charged by the white law
The children of Nonti bring their heads together
In a bid to free one of the children of Nonti.

There are no sixes and nines be one
with the children of Nonti. Truth is truth
and lies are lies amongst the children of Nonti.
For when summer takes its place after the winter
The children of Nonti rejoice
and call it proof of Truth
Truth reigns amongst the children of Nonti.

Sometimes a son rises above the others
of the children of Nonti. He explains the workings
and the trappings of white thinking.
The elders debate;
And add to their abounding knowledge
of black experience.
The son is still one of the black children of Nonti
For there is oneness in the children of Nonti.

And later, later when the sun
is like forever down;
Later when the dark rules
above the light of Truth
The black children of Nonti will rise and speak.
They will speak of the time
when Nonti lived in peace with his children;
Of the times when age did not count
above experience. The children of Nonti will stand
their grounds in the way that Nonti speared his foes
to free his black brothers from death and woes;
They shall fight with the tightened grip
of a cornered pard. For they shall be knowing that
Nothing is more vital than standing up
For the Truths that Nonti lived for.
Then there shall be Freedom in that stand
by the children of Nonti.
Truthful tales shall be told
Of how the children of Nonti pushed their will;
And continued to live by the peace
The peace that Nonti once taught to them.

Getting off the ride

I

I get off the bus ride
after long standing
listening to black voices
that obliviate the traffic noises;
A billboard overwhelms me,
Like an ugly plastic monster with fiercy eyes
it tells me what canned drink
will be good enough to quench my thirst;
I eye-mock the plastic arrogance
'Cos I know, shit, I know
I'm being taken for a ride.

II

Past this Patel's shop
The hustling efforts of these youngsters
almost urge me into seriously viewing
their imitation wrist watches,
When I know they are wanting to drain me
of the few Rands I'm still left with –
So's their brothers can get to the top drop;
And me to go on entering shops
– throwing my last Rands each time;
Ya, I know I'm being taken for a ride.

III

At the cinema house
the big poster poses a bigcrowd drawer,
I slide into the darkness;
The still blackness
is nothing but inverted blackness
cast upon imposed darkness;
I throw my eyes on the screen...
...then the long watch.
I walk out worse off,
Worse than when I mooched in;
Movies can be made to fast sell the mind
(an old warning in the family quips) like
the inflation coin at the tourist bazaar.
Again I know I've been taken for a ride.

IV

My boots jar me
as I take the corner off Grey Street
Into Victoria's busy, buzzy Victoria
Beesy Victoria's market area.
Some black mamas kneeling
their hands on the sidewalk
their second-hand clothes before them,
They kneel as if in prayer.
A white hippie bums towards them
with what shapes into a pair of
fawn corduroy jeans:

'They are fishbottomed', the aunt tilts
the deal. The seller hooks a feigned smile
with his cagey chin,
Looks like both have no choice
So the limp deal is sealed.
With unease the hippie moves off
You'd swear he's left a bomb to detonate;
I radar his moves
whilst yarning my eyes onto the mama,
the mama still on that solemn kneel
that's accompanied by sombre looks
from close range.
Where's that hippish fixer?
Into the market lanes for a blow-up;
And the black mama to scrounge a sale
after a wash of these sweaty pants
that can only be bought by some black brother
whose boss won't give him enough to afford
a pair of decent trousers.
And again I know I'm being taken for a ride.

V

I know this ride bloody well.
I'm from those squatted mothers
Those squatted mothers in the draughty air;
Those mothers selling handouts,
Those mothers selling fruits,
Those mothers selling vegetables,
Those mothers selling till dusk
in the dusty streets of Clermont, Thembisa,
Alex, Galeshewe, Dimbaza, Pietersburg.
Those mothers in dusty and tearful streets
that are found in Stanger, Mandeni, Empangeni
Hammarsdale, Mabopane, Machibisa, Soweto.
I'm one of the sons of those black mamas,
was brought up in those dust streets;
I'm the black mama's son who vomits
on the doorstep of his shack home, pissed with
concoction. Because his world and the world
in town are as separate as the mountain ranges
and the deep sea.

I'm the naked boy
running down a muddy road,
the rain pouring bleatingly
in Verulam's Mission Station;
With the removal trucks brawling for starts
Starts leading to some stifling redbricked
ghetto of four-roomed houses at Ntuzuma.
I'm the pipeskyf pulling cat
standing in the passage behind Ndlovu's barbershop

Making dreams and dreams
Dreaming makes and makes;
Dreaming, making and making, dreaming
with poetry and drama scripts
rotting under mats
or being eaten by the rats.
I'm the staggering cat on Saturday morning's
West Street. The cat whose shattered hopes
were bottled up in beers, cane, vodka;
Hopes shattered by a system that once offered
liquor to 'Exempted Natives' only.
I'm the bitter son leaning against the lamp post
Not wishing to go to school
where his elder brother spent years, wasted years
at school wanting to be white; only to end as
messenger boy.
I'm the skolly who's thrown himself
out of a fast moving train
Just to avoid blows, kicks and the hole.
I'm one of the surviving children of Sharpeville
Whose black mothers spelled it out in blood.
I'm the skhotheni who confronts devileyed cops
down Durban's May Street...
Since he's got no way to go out.
I'm the young tsotsi found murdered in a donga
in the unlit streets of Edendale, Mdantsane.

VI

I'm the puzzled student
burning to make head and tail of Aristotle
because he hasn't heard of the buried

Kingdom of Benin or the Zimbabwe Empire,
The student who is swotting himself to madness
striving for universal truths made untrue.
I'm the black South African exile who has come
across a coughing drunk nursing his tuberculosis
on a New York pavement and remembered
he's not free.
I'm the black newspaper vendor
standing on the street corner 2 o'clock
in the morning of Sunday,
Distributing news to those night life crazy
nice-timers who will oneday come into knocks
with the real news.
I'm the youthful Black with hopes of life
standing on file queue for a job
at the local chief's kraal,
This chief who has let himself and his people
into some confused Bantustan kaak
Where there's bare soil, rocks and cracking cakes
of rondavel mudbricks.
I'm the lonely poet
who trudges the township's ghetto passages
pursuing the light,
The light that can only come through a totality
of change:
Change in minds, change
Change in social standings, change
Change in means of living, change
Change in dreams and hopes, change
          Dreams and hopes that are Black
          Dreams and hopes where games end
          Dreams where there's end to man's
creation of gas chambers and concentration camps.
I'm the Africa Kwela instrumentalist whose notes
profess change.

VII

They say the Black Ghost is weak
That it is feeble
and cannot go the distance.
I say that's their wishful thinking;

The Black Ghost outmanoeuvres the wiles of Raleigh
on treacherous seas,
The ghost that steamed South Pacific trains
to Florida after Tres Castillos was not black;
Which ghost spurned the wiles of Rhodes,
Rhodes treating Black hospitality as scraps
of paper?
No, I know the Black Ghost.
It has led to many victories
In the pitch darkness of dispossession;
I can sit back and watch the screen
of Black Thoughts
In which Black success is focused.
I may not have seen Spartacus, Attila
or the Maccabee brothers for that score;
I also did not see Shaka, the Kofikarikari
or Mshweshwe, Bhambatha, for another score;
And down to those Black youths with guns
in the streets, of Watts, Harlem, Oakland.
The people of Guinea-Bissau shed their tears
for Cabral with the muzzles of their guns.
Sharpeville's Black Ghost haunts all racists,
Urges the Black people forward.
I live with this Ghost.
I've come to love this Ghost.
I live with the Black Ghost.
When I'm dumped in soulless structures
From Windhoek to Pretoria to Pietersburg
From Gugulethu to Makhutha to Ngwelezana;
Where I'm denied understanding
between me and my black brothers
according to statutes of ethnic rule;
My brothers who are caged in prisons
My brothers waiting in the dark street corners
My brothers sent to mental asylums
My brothers forced into exile
My brothers who bullshit me for a Rand
My brothers who dream of a Ford Mustang
        when they've gone to bed on empty stomachs
My brothers who'll sell their fellow brothers
        when they've lost the key to survival
My brothers who'll roll their fathers on

Friday night.
Yes, I'm made to feel motherless, fatherless, shitless
Me with enough shit in my guts to blackshit
        an officiated shit,
Me wishing for a gun
When I know some pig will wish to collar me
for the 3-Star knife I've bought at the shop
down the street.

VIII

I hate this ride.
When I know Dudu Pukwana's horn
is blowing winter out of London's black crowds;
I hate this ride.
When I dance to Miriam Makeba
Miriam Makeba's 'Jol'iinkomo' that brings back
the proud and angry past of my ancestors
by whom tribe did not be taken for nation;
I hate this ride.
When I learn no Latin from faked classics
When 2 x 2 economics shows me it's part of the
        trick – teaching me how to starve
When Coca Cola, Pepsi Cola ads, all the sweet things
        are giving me wind in the belly;
I ask again, what is Black?
Black is when you get off the ride.
Black is point of self-realization
Black is point of new reason
Black is point of: NO NATIONAL DECEPTION!
Black is point of determined stand
Black is point of TO BE or NOT TO BE for blacks
Black is point of RIGHT ON!
Black is energetic release from the shackles of Kaffir, Bantu,
                                non-white.

Sometimes there's a fall
when a brother gets off the ride,
And the fall hurts;
A fall is a hurt to every black brother.
Then I smell the jungle
I get the natural smell of the untamed jungle;

I'm with the mamba
I learn to understand the mamba
I become a khunga-khunga man
I'm with the Black Ghost of the skom jungle
I get the smell of phuthu in a ghetto kitchen
The ghetto, a jungle I'm learning to know
I hear the sound of African drums beating
to freedom songs;
And the sounds of the Voice come:
            Khunga, Khunga!
    Untshu, Untshu!
                Funtu, Funtu!
    Shundu, Shundu!!
       Sinki, Sinki!
           Mojo, Mojo!
    O-m! O--o---m! O----hhhhhhhhmmmm!!!
The Voice Speaks:
'I'm the Voice that moves with the Black Thunder
I'm the Wrath of the Moment
I strike swift and sure
I shout in the West and come from the East
I fight running battles with enemy gods
       in the black clouds
I'm the watersnake amongst watersnakes
       and fish amongst fish
I throw missiles that outpace the SAM
I leave in stealth
       and return in Black anger.
O---m! Ohhhh---mmmm! O----hhhhhhmmmmmmm!!!'

Wopko Jensma

Black bottom stomp

I

she sings her sorrows no more
no booze bottles

ma rainey dear—
my black-rim hat don't fit
my head's polluted with grief

also my *binsey poplars*
all felled, felled, are all felled
gone

mama, da bleedin moon
cuts no ice, split no dice—

bloody bustin—oh hell
if i died her
oh yea, my day'd neva eva end

II

i am here, yet nowhere
        gone lost
been at't
been walkin
been swingin
been hollerin
        it's ova
all happened right here
fast
an cuff'd
behin da bars 'f yo voice
now bear with me

bear it slow
i am here yet nowhere

III

an as da limpin chord
juxtapose ma holler

make compose maself
cleanse ma min'f god

's hard t'bear what
ma dream incantate

i hobo high, so high
on nothin but grimace

IV

i know much too much
she'll come for me: gun—
slug me in the head

alongside others dead
all just once i'll know
her core of mainline tell

V

i never called you
yet you came
i changed the lock combination
but still you entered
now i have your blood
pulsating in me as hot lead

we tell our secrets to one another
yes, nerve upon open nerve
you felled the jungle
trees that was my ultimate belief
now, as they carry the carcases
off to the sawmill
i hear your voice as mine
tolerating hell

VI `

my memories shift like sun
they're gone some—
yes, at times appear
some, as if it's none—
my memories, adrift, lost

to hell! as if your tellin
is fate—no, no one
lulls to sleep, as sense
spits up yesterday
to hell! throbbin echo—
lockjaw into four walls!

my memories splashed open
in this too steep night
your eyes agape
at my skull up a pole—
my memories, you, your blood

VII

no road has no end
no road   no end
no   end
past howl
what fire
will still my pain
my limbs split, no
none knows da word
as in begin it was
what fire
past howl
o white with light
has no road no end
in da dud
so alight
o night, what fire
past howl
in da dud
no
no road
no road has no end

In memoriam Ben Zwane

for paula

ma people, come an get ready
train's a comin
aint no room fo' sinners
we're goin all da way

i heard a word, ben
but i fear t' say 't here
tell azania
i only say 't soft, not loud

did you tumble down steps?
did you slip on a piece 'f soap?
what da hell did you do?
tell me you died 'f tb

ma people, god got ya covered
let's rail away, all stoned
'f winin'n dinin all day
gonna be great in south africa

In solitary

a man in solitary passes by
passes by me in solitary

the moon caught in tree branches

a boat with a man in it rowing

passed by me in solitary
the moon, the man, confined

it's getting late, far too late

i coined the moon, the man, free

but i remain in solitary
there's another who passes by

but i don't know him, but he is
past me confined in solitary

Lemmy knows two

I

tell me bout da others
da ones on da track, beaten
'f mind'n gut

(da jumpin pumpkin)

tell me slow
dat da goblets 'f deir eyes
turn clean white

II

i hear'm scream
                along
                small
                takings
(o pumpkin yo eye)
                haul out
                those
                stiffs
let'm gone home

Cry me a river

who's that rowing a black boat
through this black night?
who's that not sparing his arms
and rowing without end?

who's that rowing a boat
on the river without an end?
who's that not giving up hope
on a journey without end?

who's that rowing a black boat
black in the black night?
who's that hearing the slavebell
and beating the thud of his gut?

Ring da till

a call ya brudda
an a keep on callin
but brudda
ya know no tune

o lod ya white robe
o lod ya climbin on high
o lod ya shootin needle
o lod debbil an hell

& co. ltd. ma guts (pty.)
gotta business
an dough
tell toll da bell, slot
ma ringin fear—o no
o lod da stars on fire fall
o lod ma dough—o no
o lod a love
ma ol business—
ma guts & co. (pty.) ltd.

a know yu brudda
ya slap yo hands an pat
yo brudderly feet
yu wash ma soul

The pointless objects riddle

>   sumthin, yes's
>   sumthin bout'm
> it's them glumboys, grim masks
> glueboys, blueboys just dont count

top pop star tells all!
porno actress reveals all!
>   minced meet
>   t' do? be? doo
mr noah von ark's shady carnival
mrs von ark's soft lined fur
>   say-say say't
>   o say't now

amakaladi: tjarra, tjarra ad infinitum
kaffir: amaboen, amaboen ad infinitum
amaboen: kaffir, kaffir ad infinitum
tjarra: amakaladi-ladiii ad infinitum
curryball: a-hmm sanctus dominus dei...
>   :*ad lib all together now*:
amatjrblackaf bludybalshitirboenwhitrock

>   afs are great!
>   porras are nice!
now that we hate, that we once loved
but what about our children?

yr exposure to our wonderful people
our cool climate: best in the world!
>   sumthin, yes's
>   sumthin bout'm

Spanner in the what? works

i was born 26 july 1939 in ventersdorp
i found myself in a situation

i was born 26 july 1939 in sophiatown
i found myself in a situation

i was born 26 july 1939 in district six
i found myself in a situation

i was born 26 july 1939 in welkom
I found myself in a situation

now, when my mind started to tick
i noticed other humans like me
shaped like me: ears eyes
hair legs arms etc... (i checked)
we all cast in the same shackles:
flesh mind feeling smell sight etc...

date today is 5 april 1975 i live
at 23 mountain drive derdepoort
phone number: 821-646, post box 26285
i still find myself in a situation

i possess a typewriter and paper
i possess tools to profess i am artist
i possess books, clothes to dress
my flesh; my fingerprint of identity
i do not possess this land, a car
much cash or other valuables

I brought three kids into this world
(as far as i know)
i prefer a private to a public life
(i feel allowed to say)
i suffer from schizophrenia
(they tell me)
i'll die, i suppose, of lung cancer
(if i read the ads correctly)

i hope to live to the age of sixty
i hope to leave some evidence
that i inhabited this world
that i sensed my situation
that i created something
out of my situation
out of my life
that i lived
as human
alive
i

i died 26 july 1999 on the costa do sol
i found myself in a situation

i died 26 july 1999 in the grasslands
i found myself in a situation

i died 26 july 1999 in the kgalagadi
i found myself in a situation

i died 26 july 1999 in an argument
i found myself in a situation

Suspect under section a1 special

stanley turrentine, you nut! yes, 'don't mess
with mister 'T' — i agree, djy'se man van dories, 'k sê
jiggs, jiggs 'k sê, hoe's djou driving lately?
'fair to mild' — nei, 'k hoor djou met my linkeroor

i hear your tellin for truce:

o man, keep your cool, man
don't get involved! cool't
don't be heavy! cool't
groove, but don't tell you feel

this is your scene

shake to 'osibisa', baby-easy-lay
come off that homebrew dream! cool't
let'm blow your mind! cool't
groove, but don't tell you feel

now is not the time to cry...

sanctify daai cherie! sob stations stick like, hey
lyster 'k sê: 'patients are advised to remain
standing while the lift motions passengers to drop
teatrays' — a-one, a-two, a-three! dis curry-'n-ruti!

'djy'se man van dories, 'k sê: 'you're the guy from dories
     [Doornfontein], hey'
''k sê, hoe's djou driving lately': 'hey, how's your driving lately'
'nei, 'k hoor djou met my linkeroor': 'no, I'm not really listening to
     you'
'sanctify daai cherie!': 'make that baby legal!'
'lyster 'k sê': 'listen up'
'dis curry-'n-ruti': 'it's curry and ruti'

Somewhere in the middle, Sunday

for Peter Horn

I

yes, a walking cabbage just went by
     father, hallowed be thy name
what does a man look like?
when he's done that forty-four?
(after knocking back all those doubles?
(after he's gone through all those fags?
(after he's laid all those broads?
(after he's scrapped all those cars?
(after he's blown all that bread?
     lod, lemme take potatoes for potatoes
     lemme believe they can be peeled
     lemme believe they can be served
     boiled, baked, fried, mashed or chips

    lod, lemme take potato for potato
now, as my bowels breathe on the floor
now, as i hear my heart beat for piston
    father, i won't that cup o'blood
i just cannot play for time today

II

been in this cage of glass too long now
    (4 x 1 slats of glass with steel linings
    (curtainrails above, old and rusty
yes, it's a nice panoramic view of the bay
yachts, trawlers, cargo vessels from japan
    (wilko brings my curtains from pretoria
    (they're browns and reds, no stripes
the guy above drilled holes in his floor
sinking holes in the bay, wanting oil

ensor, you right: those pimpled faces...
about those masks, those sor-ghum smiles
about those x-mas hats, those red carpets
about those gallows, those skulls etc...

the cops are still looking, poking
torches into wardrobes, looking
where's that francois villon?
(he must still be upto something
he can't just get away with playing harp
on the barbed wire at the berlin wall
he can't just leave puke in the wardrobe
(he must still be upto something
the cops are still looking, poking

the guy below thuds out a daily silence
plugging up his ears, mouth, nose yeas
    (wilko's car collapsed halfway here
    (they're browns and reds, no stripes
yes, it's a nice panoramic view of the bay
yachts, trawlers, cargo vessels from japan
    (the curtainrails need bolts and nuts
    (blind & co. instals me blinds tomorrow
for today i'm pulling those blinds down

Chant of praise for the idi amin dada
recitative by his ministers

–for wolf and gündi

I

l'elephanté, mongo!

open that mouth, show your teeth
bite clean, feel the neck crack

see, he eats, he greets me
i laugh louder laugh superbrite
see, no blood, my teeth so clean

l'elephanté, mongo!

II

kiddo smashing a toy
he doesn't destroy
he perceives, percepts
he reconstructs...

III

The schizophonic splits itself, its world . . . .
Escape voices (yakkity-yak) of its conscience . . . .
Oversensitive nerves, tight as wire sinews . . . .
Gives free reign to its floodlight feelings . . . .
It's severe, wild at one, two, one, at once . . . .
It's inhibited, unrestrained, shows two face . . . .
Unintelligible cacophonic montages, it's dada . . . .

IV

PROTEST AGAINST LAW:
the law of tension
the law of precalculation
the law of reason
the law of aggression
the law of intrigue, the game...

V

VI

now read for us from the catalog mr man:

waar het hart van leeg is loopt de neus van over
HOLLAND'S BANKROET DOOR DADA

It is what the heart is empty of that makes the nose run over
HOLLAND'S BANKRUPTCY BY DADA

ja/NEIN

10. *der bruder präses der a b k bei*
    verrichtung der brüderlichkeit
16. *unerhörte drohung aus den luften*
17. *knochenmühle der gewaltlosen friseure*
19. *originallautrelief aus der lunge*
    eines 47jährigen rauchers

ROLL NICHT VON DEINER SPULE
SONST BRICHT DEIN BACKSTEINZOPF

VII

oh my!
the topheavy brainboys
my concern with my eliot-frame-of-mind
oh pollution planners & plumbers
    my everything!
but what about my subconscious attic?

VIII

now walk into the paradise of tears:
and look, look at the gallows of mirrors

and sing along

here we go loop-de-loop
here we go loop-de-lai...

---

yes/NO
10. brother Minister of the a b k at the saying
    of the service of brotherliness
16. outrageous threat from the air
17 bone mill of the non-violent hairdresser
19. original work of sound relief from the
    lungs of a forty-seven-year old

DON'T ROLL FROM YOUR REEL
OR YOUR BRICK PLAIT WILL BREAK

every-everybody wop-wop to wop's
WOPCO. INC. (grub supplies division)

die man stap die draaideur 'n kantoorblok binne
(die gebou syne: kaart transport hoeksteen)
die man suig aan 'n sigaar
(vergeelde vingers vergeelde tande)
die man het so effe sy buik gevul
(kak of betaal is die wet van transvaal)
die man is 'n belese tjekboekleser
(niks vir niks en baie min vir 'n sikspens)
die man sy pens hang verrek en swel
die man sy hare val uit sy tande vrot
die man sy trombose eelte lewer jig gee las
die man hy eet alleen in sy sesvoet graf
(hy't dit saamgeneem: sy kis soliede goud)
ek-kek-kennie anners gooi eerste steen spalk my

IX

i state, i recall, recall
kurt schwitters
jean arp
marcel duchamp
theo van doesburg
francis picabia
tristant tzara
recall, call, fukol, all

---

the man walks through the office-block swingdoor
(the building is his: conveyance and bricks)
the man sucks on a cigar
(yellowed fingers, yellowed teeth)
the man's just stuffed his gut
(shit or pay up is the law of transvaal)
the man, he's an expert cheque-book reader
(nothing for nothing and less for sixpence)
the man's gut hangs bloated and stretched
the man's hair falls out, his molars rot
his piles, his cirrhosis and gout gives him hell
the man eats alone in his sixfoot grave
(he took it with him: his solid gold coffin)
I cac-can't otherwise throw the first stone splints me

X

hey boy, i say, boy; hey mr shithead!

XI

you let me work
but you keep the bread
'oh mr richman
you dont know hard times'
you pass me wine
no way in this cage
i'm hooked; god's my witness
i better die —
wallow in wine and blood

myneer i tried
myself i cannot kill
myneer i hate

now, my hate is blind
now i'm going to love —
like hell a'm gunnu luv yu
i'll use your tools:
i'll drink the wine
but only after the bread —
god's my witness
in flesh and blood

XII

kleine verfrommelde almanak
die men ondersteboven leest
MIJN KLOK STAAT STIL
uitgekauwd sigaretteeindje op't
WITTE SERVET
de scherven van de kosmos vind ik in m'n thee

———————————

small almanac crumpled up
which people read upside down
MY CLOCK HAS STOPPED
fully chewed cigarette-stub on the
WHITE NAPKIN
I find the fragments of the cosmos in my tea

Fear freedom

after freedom struck my country
after the thousands dead
i am the only one left
the only one to know
the only one guilty
the only one to resist death
before my people's bones
before flowers of freedom country

before my people knew no nothing
before flowers were flesh
i am the only one
the only one with no gun
the only one no one suspected
the only one
after my eyes were burnt out
after remains of whitewashed bones

Letter to Thelonius

ma god, 't aint goin so good
yea, a feel da holy family
very nea' me now
ma starvin has no end

thunk, your stern face
has a wire beard and cobweb eyes
a stengun on your hip
empty booze bottles round your neck
some say, if you could drift joburg
you would stare us cold:
'thou grooveth, but thou diggeth me not'
oh melodius, like wow!
you'll let the shit hit the fan
right there
come now, don't delay

ma god, lemme sit down at yo' table
an lemme have a t-bone-steak, yes sir

Portrait of the artist

one day you got tired
tired of your soft voice
tired of being their darling

it was the opening of motau's
motau's people of violence
motau's people wanting pity

you pretended drunk
        walked up to the mike
        shouted in the mike
        patted the lady's bum
you pretended drunk

        they couldn't do a thing
call the cops? no!
kick you out? no!
        they couldn't do a thing

        they didn't want anyone to know
offer the bantu a cigar!
offer the bantu a seat!
        they didn't want anyone to know

today you've gone elsewhere
        you got sick of the mess-
        sick of the galerie-dumile
today you've gone elsewhere

one day you got tired
tired of your soft voice
tired of being their darling

I come

1

i am white and brutal
i come to you after death
and leave you completely deserted

a little tenderness
a little care
only hardens my heart

a gentle bayonet
a breeze of bullets
is the voice of my existence

i did not hear you
i won't listen
i did not hear a thing

i am white and brutal
i come to you after death
and leave you completely deserted

2

you lie hidden
in the corridors of my fear
smelling of blood

i've plucked out your eyes
i've smashed in your teeth
i've peeled off your skin

but they don't believe
– everything is just lies
but they don't believe

that i call you brother

you lie hidden
in the corridors of my fear
smelling of blood

Till no one

after miroslav holub

in sophiatown
can themba
climbs the steps
or what is left of them
he opens a door of a house
full onto the sky
and stands gaping over the edge

for this was the place
the world ended

then he locked up carefully
lest someone steal
and went back downstairs
and settled himself
to wait
for the house to rise again
for his people's legs and arms
to be stuck back in place

in the morning they found him
cold as a stone
sparrows pecking his eyes

Blue 2

!batter a fences down

enter, i coshed'm down
cup ma head in ya bloodbeat

!fence ya aint no more

baby-black ya eyes a croon
i eat ya, a lashy steak

?fence don't shadow me

aint we nobody's business?
nobody knows da trouble i see

?fence ya aint killin me

days's a down'n out, yea
zombies coon my creoletown

!fence buzz off in a blue

aint ya business, daddy-o?
ya aint foolin me no more

!batter a fences down

Confidentially yours

1

        my lord
i know my presence irritates you
i want to enter your house
and page through your thesis
and have a drink with you
and have a chat
and have a laugh
and smoke a pipe with you
and tap you on the shoulder
i am waiting at your door
i'll wait, i'll keep on waiting
        my lord

2

serowe general dealers (pty.) ltd.

a grimace this scape and you
and here could be anywhere
a khotla yonder under big tree

and old men raising hell their skulls
a woman, oh women of my village
a clear yell, a spilt otsogile
and here could be anywhere
a lone goat thorns its eyes, mud hut
a morukuru tree bleaches sun
and we are everyone

home shop is your shop – tsena!

3

    !kick that black dog

i caught some white insects
i tied them to a tin carriage

they are hauling gold from hell
they are kidding themselves silly

cause i got them all tied up
cause they graft it out all day

sometimes they go all haywire
sometime i will die laughing

    !kick that black dog

No dreams

1

stroppy kippie moeketsi
    blows a
    high-falutin –
    !no
    an heave-ho
    all blasfemis
    to-do's
    in a pea

we softly walked the holy of holies in
some MP laughs, jeers
and folds up his hands in cleanliness
    shattert we a'
    all feelin –
    !no
    dammit
    heave-ho
    dem all in a pea
    you ol
    high-falutin
stroppy kippie moeketsi

2

ah, mahlathini – mahlathini!
        hollers
           wayside da mahotella queens
      da broads pullin in
      a bunch a sailars, booze'n grub
      an we all wobblin on
      yo throat a screamin sax
        an rememba dey found
      da kids o'da broads eaten all
      – all da sailars' grub
      disgusted dey slipped away
      who's blamin da kids?
      dey had no crumb a whole week
        lets drift
        stoned da cool breeze in
ah, mahlathini – mahlathini!

3

      baybee baa-baa
        cryink
    sommer 'n oaf off's feet
        crinch sweetie
        's me
    travellin...

'sommer 'n oaf off's feet': 'just a guy off his feet'

premier wants lift to katanga – phone libertas
in national interest)
africa's on the loose –
the soldiers of peace spit bullets in gutters
in national interest)
   dja weepin baybee
     's ya dollar
      dollar brand – me
      from here

   district six
   koekenaap
   cape flats
   kakamas
   what you wish –
     whatta-hell
   forra birds?
     not me

4

   sock
   it to'm
   ave ya say-so
   yes
   talk ya mind
let the PM tantarantanta jump up and down i say
we got him in a damn nasty spot
lets pull a rag over PM tantarantanta's goggles
   what's cookin
   yes!
   we a' long out-voted
   with a
   no
   punches pulled
   we a' split
   yo excellency
   sir
   what's cookin? i says
   yu a' avin fun
   i says
   yo excellency
   sir!

In memoriam Akbar Babool

you introduced me to my first goddess
    'dis towns full a bitches
    ya wanna try one?'
afterwards we saw your home
    'loaded w'mosquitoes hea
    dey nibble ya ta pieces 'tnight'
creaky floor, a gauze door,
backyard of sand
in the middle a dagga plant
    'lets've suppa'n onion'n egg
    drive down dry bread a drop a wine'
next day the glittering town
prêgo and café com leite

me without cash later some day
you flogged the camera i stole
    'ya got trouble w'ya gal?
    listen boy, go home, juss go home'
a room in ho ling, a room at least
one with the broads, one with them
    'listen boy, go home an see ya dad
    dis place's not f'ya 't all'

sudden cash from nowhere and billy
we paint the town all bloody red
    'now prawns, boy, we a' square w'all
    square as da patten on a makapulan'
a flat in alto mae, all of it
clean bath, polished floor, wide bed
    'ya sudden luck's gonna change
    an ya laurentina'll juss be water'

for sure it happened as bad luck wanted
this time a reed hut in xipamanine
    'palish'n makov evry day
    dis reed hut, ma love, a pit walk'
sometimes akbar, sometimes billy, always i
a walk to the beach a relief, the open sea
    'ya kid gro's up, wants grub
    da kid wants ta learn letters'

yes, i remember home and drone living
cash and 8 to 5 till you are not you
    'stop dreamin, look, a'm real
    billy's sax's lost long ago'
i love my big love, my cry
the thorn bush, my life an open plain
    'akbar, 's ya, ya rotten –
    'strue, all ya said, akbar, 'strue'

sometimes now i remember you said
someone called you bloody coolie
when you asked for help
with your first heart attack
up the steps of casa elefante

Douglas Livingstone

A Darwinian preface

The crab, the clot, the muzzle or the knife:
patiently, the nocturnal terrorisms
stalk. Even the brave know hardly of rest,
aware a body's little but a glove
stretched from metatarsals to neocortex
on a siffening frame. A hand as strange
clenches on coiled lengths of fear: that old vortex
steeled by the usual mundane heroisms.
Your heart wins armour from confronting life,
yet stays unlatched, anticipating love.
Each dawn claims thanks and welcome, and gets blessed.
Perhaps the sea indeed did suckle you
through all its prisms, its diurnal range.
There is no help for it. Best buckle to.

Giovanni Jacopo meditates

(on Aspects of Art & Love)

The Poet's or Playwright's Function
Is to embark physically

Upon the Consciousness of his Generation
Not merely as the Conscience

Of his Time; nor solely to reflect
Disintegration, if Disintegration

Is the Shaker of his Time's stormy Seas.
But to anchor a Present,

Nail to its Mast
One Vision, one Integrity

In a Manner so memorable
It fills Part of a Past.

A Poet's or Playwright's Enthusiasms,
These. The proper Pursuit

For a Gentleman remains to master
The Art of delaying his Orgasms.

A morning

There were mornings following rain:
mornings of explicit languor
when the grass and hedges, near flesh
in their lushness, shone yellow in

the sun's candour; when the sea called on

its most proper blue, deploying
leached energies at the fringes.
A still woman shaded her face,
her limbs impeded by the sun.

Just such a morning when hearts, with-
out accelerating, power-
fully beat: shaking bodies from
their solitary journeys to death,

the sun's flower caught at the peak of

a respiratory apex.
The continent contemplated
movement after two centuries
of gathering its stony breath.

The sleep of my lions

O, *Mare Atlanticum,*
Mare Arabicum et Indicum,
Oceanus Orientalis,
Oceanus Aethiopicus
      save me
            from civilization
      my pastory
            from further violation.

Leave me my magics
and tribes;
to the quagga, the dodo,
the sleep of my lions.

Rust me barbed fences.
Patrol what remains.
Accept bricks, hunting rifles
and realists, telephones
and diesels
to you antiseptic main.

Grant me a day of
moon-rites and rain-dances;
when rhinoceros
root in trained hibiscus borders;
when hippo flatten, with a smile,
deck-chairs at the beach resorts.

Accord me a time
of stick-insect gods, and impala
no longer crushed by concrete;
when love poems like this
can again be written in beads.

Vanderdecken

Sometimes alone at night
lying upon your surf-ski
far beyond the sharknet

drifting on the salt-wet belly
of your mistress the black ocean,
cool under a windless moonless sky

your dangling toes you hope
not luminous from below,
dozing to the sleepy remote

mutter of shorelusting breakers
you start hearing the thrash
of bone, foam and wake;

splintering yardage and thrumming
cords; creak, groan and rattle
of blocks – and, trembling

as you lie, wet from your own death-
salt, you hear the solitary
hopeles steady cursing in Dutch.

One Golgotha

The Kill

Jerked from meditation,
a tumult of hands dragged
me to a literary death.
I fought summary bestiality:
controlling the shades within
stumbled to the crossroads.

One made prayer, one thudded
with a crucifix-haft;
I flinched from the water and garlic.

On their shoulders skulked
a terror of bloodied moons;
then the business of the mallet.

Lying in State

I await in this catafalque
fulfilment of the old lies
or a dolorous truth.

Two angels converse, rather
one: mercuric; the other
attentive, saturnine.

In my stiffenings and flakings
of leprous crackles,
I find room to consider.

The atrocity was performed
with a certain malignity:
I think my time will come.

Wheels

Cycloid dimensions gripped
the foetus
suspended where you slept.
Your mother's
young breast, the horizon, sun,
the earth and moon,
the processes which fallow loam,
the round of days
elicited a cosmos
spun out from you alone.

The experiences
and thoughts tend
to recycle themselves:
you will find
the most extensive journeys
– to inner space! –
are centrifugal, ever home
if spiralling.
Even your bright white skull is
a rosary of bone.

Mpondo's smithy, Transkei

Cold evenings: red tongues and shadows
spar under this dangerous thatch
rust-patched; one weather wall of planks;
long-limbed tools, wood, coal in smoke-dimmed stacks;
a hitched foal's harness musical.

The grindstone's rasped pyrotechnic
threatens the stopped-dead angled tip
of a stripped Cape cart that waits on
the return of its motivation;
a sudden hiss as quenched irons cool.

Two cowled purple-cheeked bellows-boys
pump, or jump for smiths or furies;
files of elders sucking pipestems,
ordered by fire's old feudalism,
squat: wrinkled jury on this skill.

Horseshoes, blades, shares and lives: all shaped
to the hoarse roar and crack of flame,
by the clang of metallic chords,
hammer-song, the anvil's undertone;
nailed to one post a jackal's skull.

Dust

The bundle in the gutter had its skull
cracked open by a kierie.
The blunt end of a sharpened bicycle
spoke grew a solitary
silver war-plume from the nape of his neck.
I turned him gently. He'd thinned to a wreck.

It was my friend Mketwa. He was dead.
Young Mac the Knife, I'd called him,
without much originality. Red
oozed where they'd overhauled him.
An illegal five-inch switchblade, his 'best'
possession, was stuck sideways in his chest.

He had been tough; moved gracefully, with ease.
We'd bricked, built walls, carted sand;
putting strength against cement-bags, we'd seize
and humpf, steadied by a hand.
I paid the regulation wage plus fifty
per cent, his room, his board. He wasn't thrifty.

We were extending the old house I'd bought.
Those baked-lung middays we'd swill
the dust with cans of ice-cold beer. I thought
he must be unkillable,
except by white men. Each night the beerhall
took him: stoned wide, he would not stall or fall.

I don't think he learnt anything tangible
from me. From him, I learnt much:
his mother, cattle, kraal; the terrible
cheat that repaired his watch; such
and such pleased a woman; passes; bus queues;
whereabouts to buy stolen nails and screws.

His wife in Kwa Mashu, a concubine
in Chesterville, a mistress
in town: all pregnant. He'd bought turpentine
but they wouldn't drink it. This
was the trouble with women. Letters came
we couldn't read. He found another dame.

He left – more money, walls half-done, him tight –
to join Ital-Constructions.
Perhaps it had been white men: I am white.
Now, I phoned the ambulance
and sat with him. It came for Mac the Knife;
bore his corpse away; not out of my life.

The recondite war on women

1   Town

The Lip they called him when he
wasn't fixing elevators.
He liked to be called it when
we were engaged, even after
our wedding, by township whores.

A romantic, though, I noticed
in our three together-years:
MacDowells' *To a Wild Rose*,
Tchaikovsky's Fifth in E Minor
(the slow part), those *Reveries* –

His old windup's in the parlour,
but none of the 78s:
not the Polovtsians, nor Siegfried's
Forest bit. Crazed from neglect
I broke them. He shrugged and left.

With the Gold City Stompers
he raped that damned sax each night.
I saw him last in uniform:
I'm off, baby, he said, south
of the border to do my bitch.

2 *Country*

Every hot still afternoon, before
the sullen evening thunderheads,
the crickets shrill. From here, the farm runs
downhill imperceptibly all the way.

The open-ended stoep frames
a coffee pot, an empty chair,
a blue-eyed woman sitting opposite
resting her arms on the plank table top.

The two front shutters need repair.
There is a troublesome kitchen floorboard.
She decides she will not wash
her long blonde matted hair today.

3 *Letter home*

'We sit before the long wade
    waiting among needle reeds;
    wind ripples the open water
    like a hand under cloth.
Something about today's date
    worries me: the Instructors
    dubbed it "The Feast of Scissors".
    laughing between themselves.
Right now, one of the Instructors
    is playing his flute quietly;
    the other threads an accompaniment
    on trembling strings:
Some song about a sampan,
    a poor tailor of Tungping,
    a saffron robe, fallen peach blossoms,
    a head shrouded in silken lace.

They will not be accompanying us.

Like a nervous father
    I cradle the latest in handweaponry,
    conscious of canvas pouches at the butt,
    my other hand holds this pen.

Previously wounded trees stand stripped,
   their bellicosity of leaves gone
   like prisoners shivering
   before the last democracy of the showers.
You once said war is the military cloak
   of male respectability
   for male infidelity:
   you should try it here for size.
My fear conjures a tracery
   of metal cutting swathes
   stitching one to another
   the banks of this river

If the killer-moon bares her face.

Take care of yourself. All my love.'

Sonatina of Peter Govender, beached

Sometime busdriver
of *Shiva's Pride*, *The Off-Course Tote*,
The Venus Trap and *The Khyber Pass Express*.
I've fathered five bright, beguiling,
alert-eyed but gill-less children.
I had to fish:
first, surf; then the blue-water marlin.
(I heard a Man once
walked water without getting wet.)
Old duels for fares:
The South Coast road – all we could get;
my left hand conning the wheel.

My last was *Dieselene Conqueror*
– night-muggings, cops,
knives, that coked and jammed injector
– right hand nursing in me a reel,
the can cracking at the start of the day,
things of the land becoming remote.
My prime as oarsman:
heroics of the offshore boat,

catching all that steel slabs of sea could express.
My porpoise-wife is gone, seeded,
spent, queen among curry-makers.
I'm old now, curt.

I've monosyllables for strangers
who stop by asking
questions while I repair my net.
Things learnt from the sea
– gaffing the landlord, the week's debt,
scooping in the crazed white shads,
twisting the great transparent mountains
past a wood blade – ?
Contempt for death is the hard-won
ultimate, the only freedom
(– cracking the cane at the end of the day –):
not one of the men I knew could float.

The waste land at Station 14

1

Agreed, Shozi,
laagers are not that cosy.
The baleful sign: 'THIS BEACH
IS RESERVED...' like a screech
or a slap '...FOR THE SOLE USE...'
set black emotions loose.

2

Shozi Bhengu, the literary star,
could pack a hall or church with raucous crowds
applauding his poems. He'd yell for shrouds
to wrap the sell-outs. He was called The Czar.
'Death,' he would roar, 'to the northern invaders,
honkies are but sacrificial goats.'
The informers listened, rehearsed their notes
– those faceless ones he slyly dubbed Darth Vaders.
Still, within his skull, the swivelling prism

of hatred, love, the racist catechism
– well-learnt – would not quite jell. 'When I am dead,'
he told his wife, 'that file under the bed
(choose the moment which looks most opportune)
holds my lyrics to the African moon.'

3

What the hell!
I might just as well
have writ the same
if Shozi Bhengu were my name.

4

Between you, Shozi, and the promised land
wavers the mirage of us.
The obstacle is not new
so there's not much to discuss.
We are the new disposables;
and, as you'll soon enough find,
so are you.
The earth you and I now know is a Karoo
of the mind
groping its way, hand over hand,
north to murderous oceans of sand.

5

Under Africa's moon there dreams a strand
older than old the ancient poets keep.
We both walk it under Africa's sun.
There, a glad profusion of brow and hand
– struck from one Mind – strikes deeper than the one
hundred or so microns which spell skin-deep;
where we could wake those old ones from their sleep
with such poems we have not yet begun
to sing: the love which Africa has fanned,
to hymn the earth perhaps, something as grand.

6

Brother-poet, verbose and gallant,
I mourn the sands that waste our talent.
For you, Shozi, this final line:
my apologies for that sign.

Isipingo

A whitewashed pane cheers the road to sand-plugged
Isipingo's river-mouth: 'Rivermouth
Singh is a fart.' ('*Au contraire, mon ami,*
I'm all heart.' His right hand palms it. His French
– broad P C Wren – 'is coming from the past;
Pondicherry; unlettered parents, dead.')
It is not the sole graffito: an 'i'
has fudged its way into each 'To Let' sign
– the town stuffed with scatological wits –
while radar scoops the air above the hill.

Rivermouth calls me Gunga. I've named him
Sinbad, which pleased him. 'I'm on the Rocs':
he spells it (– his café anchored on rocks).
'Bunny Chow? To you: 79 cents,
usually 69; but you're pure.'
Long white teeth glint villainies in the bight
of his blue-black beard. '*Mon brave... les poules* are
violins: Straddle-various,' he grins.
The Ford's rear-flap open, he peers inside:
'Your fluids look – *Mon Dieu* – nefarious.'

Three kays south, the noisome beach-pool churns as
I barge past. The Colonel (Retired), guilt-wracked
(what else, here?) and pallid, thrashes away
from three lovely nubile Asian girls
– all giggles, stretched lycra, wet slenderness.
He teaches crawl and breaststroke, risking much.
His panting hairless bulk gains turf, and heaves

towards towel and beta-blocker pack.
My own guilts nudge me, make me clumsily
wave my bottle-rack, head down, charge the surf.

Traffic interlude:
Descent from the tower

Waiting for a traffic break;
through the rear screen of the car ahead,
a toy tiger nods.
From the mangroves on the left
glides a man, a tigress from the right.
The lake glints beyond:
this turquoise mirage sustains
a Gothic tower built on an island
centred in its midst.
The man is naked, erect;
the tigress, on all fours, lifts her head,
approaches slowly.
Expression enigmatic,
she circles him, sniffing carefully.
He stands quite still; then
tentatively he hugs her,
arms about her neck. Both turn to gaze
across the silent lake.

Some daft impulse enjoins them
to merge into that blue plane between
clear sky and lake-bed.
Like most tigers, she adores
water, and she swims now with blithe strength,
great paws spreading wide,
her ears and whiskers flattened
against her skull; her submerged sleekness
to him beautiful.
Man and beast make somersaults
around one another. They surface

to splash each other.
Both panting, they reach the isle.
It is a wild and overgrown place
topped by the dark tower.
He stares across mildewed blocks:
he has seen a glimpse of shapely leg
and a makeshift hem.

He looks back, almost inclined
to return. They climb the ancient quay
slippery with moss.
'Something terrible has struck
the earth: the older I get the more
lovely the women.'
Her ears retract at the joke.
Doglike, she shakes water from her fur.
He has swung away
to confront his decision.
In vain and unseen, she lifts a paw.
Spurning jeopardy,
he starts off. Flirting ahead:
an ankle, a calf, a scrap of cloth.
Into empty rooms,
out doorways to bright sunlit
flights, shadow alternating with light;
angry growls behind.

Charging stairs, his feet take wing;
his tigress, staying close, swipes at them.
She is silent now.
He almost trips; crouching, stops
to wheel and snarl at her. She snarls back,
her yellow eyes bleak.
A truce: she will no more try
to halt him as he takes up the chase.
She bounds after him.
He slips and tumbles. At once
she springs. The fight slews across damp slabs:
his blood and his sweat.
She keeps her hooked claws sheathed, but
his disadvantage is impatience
to resume his quest.

In a niche, just above him
he sees a sword. Snatching it, he takes
a two-handed swing.

A paw skids on flags. The force
makes her recoil into her haunches.
Now, she will kill him.
As the gouting stump drains her,
he leans on the sword, waiting her charge.
Both are exhausted.
The furrows beside her eyes
shine wetly; the eyes themselves raging.
He discards the sword.
When she does not move, he spins
to spring up the final steps to find
her who went before
perched on a black throne of stone,
empty-eyed, lips parted, legs apart.
He falters and kneels
abjectly between her knees,
his aspirations in front of him.
This must be the Source.

'God of the Holocaust heaps;
of carcharhinids, carcinomas
in children, floods, quakes;
of grief, Down's syndrome', he prays,
'cruelty in men, leukæmias –
make poems within me.'
Slowly, with savour, she spits.
He stands, leans over, rips off her shift.
Flame wreathes her white thighs.
He turns to stagger away.
An arrow flogs past his ear. One flight
down, he finds the paw.
Racing the fresh gory trail,
he finds her; binds the stump with the skirt;
helps her down the steps,
the tower cracking around them.
He concentrates on the weakened cat.
At last: the cool deeps.

The blue lake, stauncher of blood:
he knows it will heal his earthbound love;
it will heal them both.
In the water, he swims down,
tugs off the cloth, presses paw to stump
where it seems to knit.
He surfaces. They swim on.
Her strength grows. She paws his head – *that* paw;
then calmly ducks him.
Reaching shore they pause to watch:
the tower is crumbling; too far away
to be heard, it dies.
He kisses her on the nose.
She licks his cheek, eliciting blood
– her tongue like sharkskin.
It is not over for them:
they will meet here on this bank again
to spar in the mud.

Lionel Abrahams

Thresholds of tolerance

In this climate of storms
the streets shine with tears.
Let those who have eyes
let those who have anger
set strong faces toward the streets.

I turn inside my room
turn, turn.
If I have strength
if I am blessed with vision
I shall possess my private life.

That poet's naked nerves
thunder:
there are days when even beauty
appals him,
he turns his paintings to the walls.

But I, inside my room
I can't be frightened.
I choose nightmare drawings
and paintings that are full of grief.
Behind my door, in the quiet,
I hunt my private life.

Dry self-portrait

the residence of truth
is houghton ridge

i have said my say

my thoughts buzz
round all the things i have
i own growth units shares
machines art works and books
two pairs of specs black friends
a magazine my name
is known to x and y my views
are sought my jokes my
sympathetic ear

my voice drags when i'm bored

and i dine out
on anecdotes about
a or b or me delightful truthful
tales who wants my
nice fresh anecdotes

j's poems and theories of prof m
i can explain i've said
my say my say about that lie
or this mistake the
well-intentioned make
why can't they see

i've said i've said
truth lives in fordsburg dip
the guru knows
yet all i needed say was need
your hands my half love let's
touch hands or core and core
where are you sore
say where you are sore

i've said my say
where can truth stay

Our way of life
(A situationist jingle)

We Europeans
in the land of Baas
carry the vote
and not the pass –
yes, we're all right: we're all white.

A has been raided,
B has been bugged,
C has been censored,
D has been jugged –
all all right: they're all white.

E, uncharged,
has sat a while;
F, more lucky,
is on trial –
but they're all right: they're quite white.

G was denounced
as provocateur-spy;
now H is suspected,
perhaps also I –
as well we all might be: we're all white.

J got provoked
to go slogan-painting:
she sat six months
and she was eighteen,
but came through all right, being white.

K got twelve years,
L got five,
M was let out
while still alive
to die all right: all three were white.

N disappeared
for ninety days.
O learnt the rule
that caution pays:
a fright's a fright although you're white.

P can't teach, Q can't preach,
R and S can't talk to each
other, T can only to his spouse,
U can never leave her house –
but they're all right: they're all white.

V got kidnapped,
W, banned
X got a brick
On which to stand –
still, they're all right: they're all white.

Some of us leave
and some lie low,
but are we intim-
idated? No!
It puts us right to know we're white.

I got visited
Y got slanged
(small-time troubles)
but Z got hanged –
yet he was all right: he was white.
Yes, we're all right: we're all white.

After winter '76

Jacaranda purple lends
a regal show to sunlit well-off streets,
burning and smoking among roofs,
splashed bright across gutters.
The blossoms, each a little air
sealed in a velvet trumpet,
make silent fanfares
and fall whole.
They burst underfoot as we pass.
Predicting their tough seeded legacy,
history should make something
of their present soft reports.

Out of illness

1

O how I know all the answers,
o how I am trusted!

Curled up here in the shade
I try to remember delight.
Come back, o come back.
Words could do it, and faces,
and prospects for the flesh.

O how I loved the chance of being known
for some kind of truth or usefulness,
a staunchness on behalf
of what was imperilled and precious.
O how full I could be with a piece of your art,
feeling sure I could tell,
or of my own, believing a gift had come.
O sweets and toys and jokes,
o bioscope, o brandy and repartee and yarns,
o wheeling birds, o visitors,
o even the subtle breath of autumn.
I am no Buddhist but I seem released
from all desires. No. I want
release from the body's treacheries,
to be engaged by something else,
by the desire of passion,
by affection and curiosity,
or at least let me be engaged
by the anger that lurks behind my dreams.
Come back, o come back.
Until I am filled with lust my head is unclear –
let no one trust me,
ask me for no answers.

2

Why do I keep looking past the image –
into the machinery of time?
If the image is lovely and mild

why don't I rest on it?
That is why I fail as a poet –
I am compelled toward the
absolute fact, like a sort of
insurance policy. I can't let
the image have its way,
I can't play
or free associate.
Look at those who get things done,
the creators of fine living things
that increase the world:
they aren't so damned insistent
or careful or accurate,
somewhere they trust what comes up
before the eye or the mind's eye
or the heart's eye,
and they know how to
give over and let flow.
But never mind poetry,
which after all 'changes nothing' –
this X-ray trick of mine,
dissolving all the firm surfaces
or lovely feathery ones
for the sake of the certainty behind,
yields me nothing
but a squalid bit of grief
and dread.

3

Books, upholstery,
curtains, trees under sunlight,
birdsounds and kitchen sounds,
why don't you embrace me
after the gray of the hospital?
Why do you leave this core inside me
like a metal obelisk for war?
I have looked into the mad face
of my century. Madness
is not wild and unpredictable,
madness is rules, routines, straight lines,
honest nakedness about necessity,

order, order, while the sky bursts.
I have looked into God's face,
planes of grey metal that can't move.
Every sober adult receives this robot god:
march march march march bing, the line
straight as a corridor through nineteen departments.
The warship casts off to cheers,
tears, music, jokes, a human tradition,
and inside each adult the blank god
march march march march bing.
There is no other direction
this is the century of machines
the century that knows the century that bursts the sky
this is the century that follows through
march march march march bing
inside each adult the core
of metal machine that must do one thing
the core that cannot be embraced.

4

A woman phones at eight in the morning
to ask that I love her a little.
I can't recall the pleasure
that once used to pass between us:
I promise her nothing.
To the man who came to say
I am precious to him,
I respond with criticism.
I listen to poems and stories
with the restraint of cold thought.
Hiss and rumble of the machinery
blocks from my ears the music of things.
Have I forgotten how to rejoice
in the nervous love-dance of the dog,
the tragic gossip of the pigeons,
the rich fall of the sunlight?
Does honey lie inert on my tongue?
Is it because the nerve of my sex
has been touched by metal and numbed
that now I don't know how to love?

Don't say it

The walls have gooseflesh
Don't say it
The water shrinks
The morning darkens
Don't say it don't say it
What though the perspective ends
by throttling the air, what
when the innards are filled with sand?
Don't say it.
Don't say it unless
the night yields up your head
or the broken sand sustains your foot.
Don't say it unless you find
music under the nails that scraped the door.

Family man

In the family I eat.
In the family I can call
for rescue at midnight.
When I was struck down the family
bore me up, contained me
like an unborn child.
My weakness is my strength in the family.
When I would be rash or proud
the family shows me practical wisdom.
The family fills in my forms
with suitable assertions.
Consulting no sentiment, no tidal affections,
without reserve or conditions, the family
cares that I am clean and safe.
Though I keep guilty secrets,
steal a space for decisions,
make disloyal alliances with strangers
and smuggle in danger and love –
the family, owning half my name,
keeps me, keeps me and never
questions my maverick voice
or investigates
my ingrate face.

A stone stood in her house

A stone stood in her house.
The stone lay in her bed.
Under the rain of her words
the stone gave out nothing.
Her child moved about the stone,
wishing this, wishing that.
The stone said: 'Mine is mine.'
She threw herself on the stone:
'Open! Give! Move!'
Stunned in her skull,
her back bruised,
she went beyond honey,
beyond bread,
beyond water.
The stone contented her.

Spring report

Schizophrenic Africa for us enacts a Spring.
The wind disturbs leaves, shadows, doors.
A dog weeps at a shut gate.
A grief-stricken woman
stands ironing in the kitchen
talking quietly about other things.
On the telephone a visitor from abroad
whose face I have never seen
accuses me of malice.
A young girl teases
new scar tissue from her temple.
The dreamy boy visiting her
is a conscript on leave.
The letter with money
brings me news of one more divorce.
The radio's bulletin of outrage and threat
also announces a prize.
So it goes, tidings every hour
but not on the hour –
there is no knowing when,

nor what the next message may contain.
'Excursion into music' pours
into the Rosh Hashonah forenoon
'Jesu, Joy of Man's Desiring',
comforting none in this house.
We can open the gate for the dog.

Privacy

Surgery has cut me back
to the beginnings of things.
The individual adult bourgeois,
wealthy in choices and secrets,
respectful of the neighbour's privacy,
has had it.
Where I sleep the nurse-aid sleeps near.
I eavesdrop perforce
on the muttered racing commentary
of her intense prayers
and the squeaking bedsprings of the voiceless frenzy
she rides through with her man –
the same who makes my room his thoroughfare.
I can't play my radio at midnight,
and if I do not keep the stillness of sleep
but try the tune of a thought with my voice
she thinks I am addressing her.
My need grants her the private parts of my life.
Perhaps I am learning something
about those to whom no private life's vouchsafed,
collectivist citizens, soldiers, prisoners,
migrant workers in their local hostels,
the crowded ubiquitous poor?
But the nurse-aid's endearments and fondlings
claim too much, and I rail at her.
I want to order the work of my mind.
I want to sleep with a woman I love.
I want an end of this kind of aloneness
and to be alone.

Winter report

The child is silent.
The beloved friend is silent.
My dreams and my songs are silent.
One pane of my window frames an aloe's head,
a tropical image in the winter air,
grey-green as stone
a tangled rose of fleshy scimitars
or a shrapnel-burst in some vegetable war
with seven flames of flower above.
The aloe, however, is silent as sculpture,
while I am mobile, voluble, quite approachable:
telephone on my desk, chairs tête-à-tête,
the kettle round there, the liquor cupboard near.
Comfortable, I talk, read, scribble instructive marginalia,
display no confusion of spikes,
no efflorescence of defiant heat.
But at times I grow restless with this truce,
at times of silences.
The silence of the child is terrible.

To Halley's Comet

Good evening, little visitor.
We know you're there, it's in the news.
But who'd have thought you'ld be so shy,
so hard to spot, among the stars?
Who'd have thought, instead of streaking through,
flashing that famous double tail,
autographing the prophetic sky,
you'ld do an elusive Garbo act?
Perhaps it's because, this time round
you find we know too much
about a dirty undense snowball
only as big as Table Mountain, say,
that only shines because the sun
lends it a bit of common light.
You've lost your ancient awesome mysteries
your sign-dimension that could move

the old Wise Men, King Harold and Mark Twain.
And so you shrink and hide among our city lights,
claiming a different subtlety.
I like it, in a way: it's less fun
but somehow more moving, that after all
you're so minute and fragile:
you enter our domestic patch of sky
not barging heavy like some line steamer,
sky-bus or iron-railed train,
but lightly, chancily, only just making
your long, lonely orbit
by the skin of your momentum.
We should applaud like mad
that you make it again on time.
You've shed the scary Nostradamus mask
and now drop by, like some private rare Aunt Maud
between prodigious travels,
merely to show yourself and check our face.
No more the fortune-teller, dearest Aunt,
by never getting lost along
those shifting paths of lonely space,
arriving as expected after a lifetime's lapse,
you give us your gift, allow that we
achieve a stroke of prophecy.
We thank you, little comforter:
the dark potent emptiness ahead
contains one probable smear of light.

Thoughts on Johannesburg's centenary
(while by the Jukskei River at Broederstroom)

There is no city as old as a river,
as old as this minor stream
whose millennia have sculpted the veld.
The wiser cities lie down with great rivers
to learn what rivers teach of time,
or with the timelessness of seas;
but my city's mazed metal of hurried streets
has buried the small white waters.

What if my wandering clan had given me
one of those old wise cites to be born in?
I would have claimed that borrowed ancestry
of mellow stones and streets, embraced
the longings and learning of that home,
spelled my name in its memorial marks.
Instead they gave me to raw spawn of payable lode,
attracting loose acquisitive pioneers,
the hungry and threatened, chancers and transients
– swelling by gross promises and harsh divisions
over unhistoric farms and hills.

Born but never Native here (of Europe-stranger kin,
that skin), I've known no other place to claim.
Heir to the Book, I find and lose my living myths
more in these too changeable streets.
I learned to spread from hollow roots a patched familiarity:
time gave my stories to some names and contours;
certain settings of my years, my selves, won my affection,
enrolled me in a Masonry of esoteric love.
I belong with the unbelonging, and this world
of second generation strangers, all its cheap renewal,
gives me my only earthed tradition,
all prospect of a self-built meaning I can claim.

How can you love what changes too swiftly,
too swiftly changes and changes again?
A river is momently different, and daily,
but the slow living banks hold the shape of memory –
the self can stay while the river runs
and we can love the river.
But these streets hardly
survive their shouting rivers of traffic;
this place owes too little to time,
too much to appetite and rage
and guilty self-contempt –
it eats and tears itself… renews… renews…

A man stays naked at the dumb mouth of the cave,
shivering like a dog beneath thunder –
a man and his streets are disposable trash
if the town does not bequeath to his passing eye
old shapes told about in tales,
histories held visible in shapes
that he knows will still be seen beyond his time.

If all who must leave
take their insights and go,
take the innocence they will not lose
and go,
and the rage burns out,
and the gold gives out,
yet the Name of the city endures –
this place may draw together, discover
the richer reasons of its century,
may hear the singing of its hundred-year-old course.

The writer in sand

He is, perhaps, none of my business
I'm not of His faithful, none of His flock,
no candidate for His mysterious rescue
of my dubious undying part.
'I have,' I told a pavement proselytiser
who asked if I was Saved,
'made my own arrangements, thanks.'
I'd leave Him to Himself and His,
I do believe, if He'd leave me alone.
But one way and another He goes on
being broadcast into my days:
Resurrectionist that He is,
He keeps coming up.

So what I want to say is, Yes,
I like some things about Him, like His style
in parables and miracles and jokes
(the first stone – Caesar's coin –
mud in the blind man's eyes –
the cripple's carried bed...
Blessed are the clowns, they'll
straighten out the world).
I like, too, that penchant of His
to spin His Peters and Marys,
into tremendous situations.
And look at His own on the hill between thieves!

But here's my But:
some of His adorers overstate the hell of it,
that cruel end, as though excess of agony
itself were holy or the cause of holiness,
and no non-God had died as hard and long.
Well, I know a list who suffered
(suffer, are still suffering) worse –
Job, say, or some of Hitler's Jews,
Biko, and that friend I watched
writing toward death in a hospital bed –
a few whose many deaths are drawn through years.
Pain is common squalid stuff I won't admire.
For me the News is not His piteous stations,
not the way He hung on spikes,
sweated and thirsted and despaired.
Spare me the Passion of the Sufferer,
that bleeding Man of Sorrows line!

I open to the writer in the sand,
the carpenter of metaphor, washer of feet,
the teacher, the healer, the wit,
the queller of shoals and winds,
the feeder, the yarner, the relationship-man
who took time with Martha's sister,
indulged an extravagant girl's
pouring of balm and her hair over His feet,
called back Lazarus to favour some dear friends,
and reminded those awe-stunned parents
to feed their resurrected child.

Flesh

Busy in my skin in my house, I receive
rumours and news. Again and again I hear
about too much death, too much pain,
too much emptiness, the culpabilities,
relentless causes and terrible ends.
Hearsay comes muffled, distorted,
diminished through the walls of my house.
Busy in my safe place, the attention I pay
takes the form of distraction.
Busy in my safe skin, I attend
with half an ear or heart –
because my skin, from my side,
after all is no safe place.
The walls of my house contain
sufficient travail,
the floor lies ready to bruise me,
beat out my breath. Health, safety,
time for work are not vouchsafed.
I must carve them out of each slippery
hard-textured day, must grapple
with the knotted minutes for those luxuries:
my bare subsistence, a glint of meaning.
This is why, for all I have heard,
I remain, you could say, aloof;
in practical terms, you could say,
ignorant of the struggle.

To the idealistic killers

Brothers in sacrifice, hail!
How lean and pure you are,
you strict kings of thought!
Nothing tempts or confuses you.
Neither pain nor questions
spoil your certainty.
You know like magicians and poets
the way of transmutation:
anything can transcend

its primitive self to become
a legible sign in your revelation.
Your alchemy reads fire,
brands flesh to order,
stirs the muddy world to your ideal.

Fat and full of doubt
we salute you, we who take
things for what they are,
hoping to suck some hope
from some bone of compromise,
some comfortable sweet justice
out of some gradual
lollipop of change.
We salute you, acknowledging
that probably you will win,
probably you will
inherit the world
and all its dead.

Agnostic's funeral prayer

Certain of no definition, we few
who by blood, law, affection or duty
are linked to one who has died,
assemble in a naked place
to contemplate once more
the recurring mystery
which any familiar death
presses upon our attention.
One of us, of our very selves,
has become mere dissolving matter,
filth of which earth has to cleanse us.
And all we acknowledged as life,
that person's identity,
recedes into pure recollection,
stuff much like dream and illusion
which only expendable flesh
made real, real as ourselves.

'*Cogito ergo sum*' seems no affirmation
but question, petition
to be not shut alone
in the only mind,
that coldest perdition,
o, not deluded by all the lights
and pictures of thought.

Origin of all origins
or destiny of all destinations,
Transcendent Idea, defiant
of all definition,
we invoke You now, as whenever
mortality strikes our fragile
manifestation,
to help us bear the strangeness
of our awareness, the terror
and riddle of what we seem
to be and become.

Empty of knowledge
we rest the newly dead with You.
God of man's making
include the lost beloved
and us in Your meaning.

Song for the new order

(*Villanelle*)

Seek salvation in the crowd.
Joy is tired and songs are stones
and loveliness is not allowed.

Justice, grown simple, quick and loud,
is bawled in happy children's tones.
Let's seek salvation with the crowd.

Language is loosened: poets are proud
to drum their lines with gray fools' bones,
and loveliness is not allowed.

Mourning dances, rage is vowed
like love, like tender care intones:
'Come, seek salvation with the crowd.'

The poor possess, the rich are cowed,
let go their stuff. Who knows who owns
whose property? It's not allowed.

Chants and wishes turn the cloud,
and no one will call in the loans.
Then seek salvation with the crowd
though loveliness is not allowed.

At revolution's end

The mild-eyed white-haired wedding guest
carries behind spectacles and pallor
huge secrets of fragility and power.
Astute, patient strategist of an apocalypse,
he is at last a Cabinet Minister
in the achieved glorious government,
at last is tasked to build,
but has to formulate a policy
to meet approaching death.

I know about him more perhaps than most
(more than he guesses) yet not enough
of his dangerous history – what sacrifices
might his perfect purpose justify? –
to share the certainty of those who love,
or those who fear and hate him.
Besides who-knows-how-many deep debates
and plots, his serial of missions under cover,
specified bullets and labeled bombs,
he has survived the great dialectical disappointment:
retaining his visionary certainty,

the Jewish atheist (dreamer or schemer)
has claimed an armed judgemental Jesus Christ
as warrior in his People's war.

What – in our skin or genes, schemes
for survival, teachers' creeds,
the streets we've lived in, scars
of the years, secrets of the couch –
elects the rhetorics that direct
and rouse our different hearts?
This politician's passion of faith
shifts and hammers history's mass,
and sends down states, while mine
dictates the fall of syllables.

We could be neighbours, brothers,
but the poems we each can hear
are hieroglyphic to the other.

He has been sitting at this table
remote at the core of a silence
which even his magnificent daughters
seem reluctant to breach.
A white shadow covers him,
a cold flame slowly consumes
his material life.

He rises and walks in my direction.
I'm holding my table with a boastful anecdote,
and when his eye catches mine and he asks,
with a curious urgency, 'Are you
saying something to me?' I wave him
aside. He swerves away, and I slowly
grow to know that now
when he is weakest and strongest
something might have been spoken.

Ingrid de Kok

To drink its water

1

Home is where the heart is:
a tin can tied to a stray dog.

The only truth is home truth:
preserves on the winter shelf.

Those who carry their homes on their backs
live for hundreds of years,
moving inch by inch from birth to lagoon.

2

Beside the beaten path
to the veld where I once played,
dry riverbed and unwashed clothes
grey lizards on the rocks.
My shadow squats in the shade of a thorn
where children sift and store
the remnants of corroded bins.
Over the path, the rocks, the tree,
marauding sky, fiercer than memory.

3

In a hot country
light is a leper,
water the eye of a goat
on the fork of an honoured guest.

The tap in the camp drips onto the bone of the gum.

And those in the cool green houses,
owners of the sweet white water,
owners of the bins and wells,
die swollen, host and guest of a herd of eyes
washing within them.

4

To return home, you have to drink its water,
in a drought, you have to drink its water,
even from the courtyard well,
the water blossoming in the gut,
or brackish, from a burning trough,
flypaper on your tongue,
pooling your hands,
bending when you drink.

5

Home is where the heart is:
husk of heat on the back.

The sky enters into the skin,
the sky's red ants
crawl over the shoulders.

This bending body is my only body.
I bend and drink
the shadow in the water.

Leavetaking

We are not loving women, having lived long
or intending to. Daughters grow old together.
Sons die, watched over by women.
This isn't Greece but it might as well be.
We move as if robed in black, all widows,
all clean, all careful.

I had one aunt who died young.
They laid her out in white.
She was buried in the late afternoon.
Afterwards I walked back to the house.
My grandmother was waiting,
and the others had prepared food.

This is a dream I have:
I die old but my mourners are older.
They remember my hands and my mother.
My coffin is painted with wild white roses.
There is no keening at all.

At this resort

Tropical plants fringe the sea,
voluptuous branches, heavy with steam and heat
rot onto the moving dunes.
In front of the verandah here
berries swell, red,
crack open like eggs,
their seeds glow poison,
irradiate, glow red.
But for all we know they might have healing properties,
nourish birds, oil flaccid feathers:
they might have saved us.

Really, there is no secret in the view.
I put it there.
No loss at all but landscape, landscape.
The tree bears nothing
that cannot be identified.
The rule of thumb is:
do not eat what even birds avoid.
But here we cannot tell which are the birds.

At the edge of the resort,
beyond the shop, dining room,
bowling greens, the children's trampoline,
the stars dip their wicks
into the waxen fever trees
and shadowy men and boys throat
across the low lagoon.

So lose again a father, lover, son,
to the dark sand
that no one cares to tread upon
unless it is the only pathway
to the rocks and then the hills.

And all along the broken water,
women wardens stand
shaking hands forever at the church door,
greeting the mourners in their dark lapels,
while the coffins heave themselves into the sea.

My father would not show us

Which way do we face to talk to the dead? Rainer Maria Rilke

My father's face
five days dead
is organized for me to see.

It's cold in here
and the borrowed coffin gleams unnaturally;
the pine one has not yet been delivered.

Half-expected this inverted face
but not the soft, for some reason
unfrozen collar of his striped pyjamas.

This is the last time I am allowed
to remember my childhood as it might have been:
a louder, braver place,
crowded, a house with a tin roof

being hailed upon, and voices rising,
my father's wry smile, his half-turned face.

My father would not show us how to die.
He hid, he hid away.
Behind the curtains where his life had been,
the florist's flowers curling into spring,
he lay inside, he lay.

He could recall the rag-and-bone man
passing his mother's gate in the morning light.
Now the tunnelling sound of the dogs next door;
everything he hears is white.

My father could not show us how to die.
He turned, he turned away.
Under the counterpane, without one call
or word or name,
face to the wall, he lay.

Shadows behind, before

Sky, almond and chalk,
fields bleached with old use,
the highway a silver arrow
through the heart of it all.
If I keep travelling this way
will I know when I've reached the site,
knowledge trickling through my fingers
my hands so full of its soil?

There are two myths of possession here:
the myth of the exile, wanderer,
carrying loss like a bomb under his coat,
a load of winter wood on his back,
mercenary of his own heart's plunder;
and the myth of the householder,
partisan of familiar fields,
who builds his past from mud and water
and his future with the same.

No matter if he visits a valley, the exile
watches from a copse on a windless hill.
But a native in his own place cannot afford
to speculate on the distance to his father's barn.
Each in silence walks a pathway
to a pond that barely moves,
but one turns his back on his own long shadow
and one watches his shadow lead him deep into winter.

In this chill evening ride
the houses buckle into the road's long belt.
Behind a window a woman watches me pass,
matching my eyes as they snatch and drop her.
She sees me, promised unknown distance,
free or urgent to be travelling away;
I see her draw water from a deep metallic well,
I see her candles for the dead.

Dream of a trophy

In my dream you are a mendicant
carrying an onyx bowl.
I feed you violets and small roasted rats
and you sing for your sorrows
and eat out of my hand.

The weight of your cape is the weight of this dream
and is tied to your neck by an emerald clasp.
But your body beneath is battered and thin
like a sliver of glass or ice.

I polish the dents in your dream body
and see myself there, polishing.
Your collarbone gleams like pewter.
I could hang your cheeks on the wall, like plates.
You are what I want you to be, at night.

Visitor

When you turn to me, carrying your weight on your side
like a gypsy with a pail, I must stroke you cleverly,
gently, taking care to be silent: sounds carry.

You are a guest here, and your pain is unfamiliar to me
even when you turn like this into my hospitable hands
and I have to call you my own.

On a still afternoon, you visit your request on me
that I cannot answer, cannot refuse.
You are thinner than I remember.

This thing we learn from others

From the hitchhiker whose head
falls against your shoulder in his sleep
as you swerve in the dark rain,
from two small boys waving
at a Safari Tour bus,
from others, that stowaway for instance,
who gave himself up because
from his hiding place
he couldn't smell the sea,
and from people who bury their dogs
in gardens, at night,
remembering the date until they are old.

They say if your mother held you
on her right side, head in the moist curve
of her arm, you are lonely,
and if she held you on her left,
her breast breathing into your ear,
you are lonely.

To be thus
is what we should have expected.

Only, at neap tide,
its moon just a glance
over the wet uncovered miles of sand,
the rocks white and black micra in the dark,
and waves which had buried themselves
at our feet, now trebling quietly
far out there
made us come close
to the fire on the beach,
made us think it possible
to stay that way,
scooping warm coals into the heart.

Small passing

For a woman whose baby died stillborn, and who was told by a man to stop
mourning, 'because the trials and horrors suffered daily by black women in
this country are more significant than the loss of one white child'.

1

In this country you may not
suffer the death of your stillborn,
remember the last push into shadow and silence,
the useless wires and cords on your stomach,
the nurse's face, the walls, the afterbirth in a basin.
Do not touch your breasts
still full of purpose.
Do not circle the house,
pack, unpack the small clothes.
Do not lie awake at night haring
the doctor say 'It was just as well'
and 'You can have another.'
In this country you may not
mourn small passings.

See: the newspaper boy in the rain
will sleep tonight in a doorway.
The woman in the busline
may next month be on a train

to a place not her own.
The baby in the backyard now
will be sent to a tired aunt,
grow chubby, then lean,
return a stranger.
Mandela's daughter tried to find her father
through the glass. She thought they'd let her touch him.

And this woman's hands are so heavy when she dusts
the photographs of other children
they fall to the floor and break.
Clumsy woman, she moves so slowly
as if in a funeral rite.

On the pavements the nannies meet.
These are legal gatherings.
They talk about everything, about home,
while the children play among them,
their skins like litmus, their bonnets clean.

2

Small wrist in the grave.
Baby no one carried live
between houses, among trees.
Child shot running,
stones in his pocket,
boy's swollen stomach
full of hungry air.
Girls carrying babies
not much smaller than themselves.
Erosion. Soil washed down to the sea.

3

I think these mothers dream
headstones of the unborn.
Their mourning rises like a wall
no vine will cling to.
They will not tell you your suffering is white.
They will not say it is just as well.
They will not compete for the ashes of infants.
I think they may say to you:

Come with us to the place of mothers.
We will stroke your flat empty belly,
let you weep with us in the dark,
and arm you with one of our babies
to carry home on your back.

Transfer

All the family dogs are dead.
A borrowed one, its displaced hip
at an angle to its purebred head,
bays at a siren's emergency climb
whining from the motorway.
Seven strangers now have keys
to the padlock on the gate,
where, instead of lights, a mimosa tree
burns its golden blurred bee-fur
to lead you to the door.

'So many leaves, too many trees'
says the gardener who weekly
salvages an ordered edge;
raking round the rusted rotary hoe
left standing where my uncle last
cranked it hard to clear a space
between the trees, peach orchard,
nectarine and plum, to prove
that he at least could move
the future's rankness to another place.

Forty years ago the house was built
to hold private unhappiness intact,
safe against mobile molecular growths
of city, developers and blacks.
Now rhubarb spurs grow wild and sour;
the mulberrries, the ducks and bantams gone.
In the fishpond's sage-green soup
its fraying goldfish decompose the sun,
wax-white lilies float upon the rot.
And leaves in random piles are burning.

Townhouses circle the inheritance.
The fire station and franchised inn
keep neighbourhood watch over its fate.
The municipality leers over the gate,
complains of dispossession and neglect,
dark tenants and the broken fence.
But all the highveld birds are here,
weighing their metronomic blossoms
upon the branches in the winter air.
And the exiles are returning.

Ground wave

Just below the cottage door
our moraine stairway of lemon trees,
strelitzia quills and oleander shrub
steps to the sea and deeper terraces.
The warming wind, concertina on the slope,
coaxes open the bulbul's throat,
the figtree's testicular green globes
and camellia's white evening flux.

Behind the house we feel
the mountain's friction against our backs.
Deep fissures are predicted by the almanac,
earth and trees heaving to the shore.
Scorpions come in at night
for cool killings on the flagstone floor.

Still life

The woman is wild.
The child has grown
away from this place
to a view of its own.

The woman is still.
The child has gone
behind the hill
foreign moons shine on.

The woman's alive.
The child was led
from summer ground.
The child is fled.

The woman yields the cavity,
renounces daily care,
grants the earth its gravity,
the sky its horizontal stare.

At the Commission

In the retelling
no one remembers
whether he was carrying a grenade
or if his pent up body
exploded on contact with
horrors to come.

Would it matter to know
the detail called truth
since, fast forwarded,
the ending is the same,
over and over?

The questions, however intended,
all lead away from him
alone there, running for his life.

Ecotone

On the west, thornveld, teeth on trees,
and on the eastern plateau
savannah grassland, a lion's mane.
We tracked animal shapes,
fixing time and place
until the light swallowed its tongue
and the rasping of hunting and hiding
choked us in the dark.

But here between, on this thin strip,
the static of insects underfoot
– you wouldn't call it no-man's land –
migrant birds alchemize,
morning mist sieves its cool alluvial spray
and one thing becomes another, imperceptibly.

Mending

In and out, behind, across.
The formal gesture binds the cloth.
The stitchery's a surgeon's rhyme,
a Chinese stamp, a pantomime

of print. Then spoor. Then trail of red.
Scabs rise, stigmata from the thread.
A cotton chronicle congealed.
A histogram of welts and weals.

The woman plies her ancient art.
Her needle sutures as it darts,
scoring, scripting, scarring, stitching,
the invisible mending of the heart.

My mother's house hold

My mother held us to her.
This made friends chafe and sting,
or want her for their own.

There we four were, dragging our feet
backwards and forwards to her love,
trying to keep a secret of ourselves,

while the house filled up with
other people's children.
Perhaps she stole them away.

Now there are more,
those children's children,
an undertow of love.

Watching them, she plays
the same tune I heard at seven:
early anarchic Nat King Cole.

Tender, fatalistic,
ur-mothering,
learnt between the wars.

My mother says it's harder
to love a happy person than a sad one.
They need you so much less.

She says she'll put a plastic bag
over her own head
when she wants to die,

not rely on squeamish us
to do the right,
the braver thing.

My mother holds us to her.
This makes friends chafe and sting
and want her for their own.

The talking cure

Sometimes a man walks away from a window
just as light splinters the screen.
Sometimes a diver hired to resurrect beauty
secretly buries the brightest pearl.
Sometimes the story keeps winding back to the same place.
And who would believe the gristle and lung
in our short conversations?

Mouthing under water
wetly jewelled words,
we are acrobatic aquanauts
in a chest of swords.

The ravine between looks ordinary,
except for its shining edge –
handrest, footrest, headrest, the heart's ledge.
To choose not to love requires a kind of courage.

Houdini in a set of locked boxes,
suspended between walls,
between transfixed watchers
and his own pent breath,
suddenly, seen by all,
unlocks himself into the light.
And though we know it is a trick,
we speak the miracle it could have been.

Here too: riddle, spiral, ruse,
a ridge of words that look like acts.
On a suspension bridge,
we tightrope into talk:
silver, dancing alphabets
strung with loops and hoops,
arabesques of words on a swaying net.

Thus are we cured of touch
and the imagined mobility of love,
where my tongue would move
in the centre of your mouth.

Text of necessity

One by one
the small refusals
add up to a life.

Each returning home
is a scanter triumph.

You give and gain
scrupulous care, scrupulous blame,
won and lost and then reclaimed

to wear like polished bone:
an amulet to ward off and to hold

the present and the past,
their vacancies and weight,
and early outlines in white light.

What you want
becomes a set of words,
mirrors in your mouth.

Transpose this into necessity,
or make it plain

when you stifle, as you rename
the stirring of some
unscheduled love or pain.

Salamander

Marquisite, false diamond,
most desirable cheap snake:
the lucid silver of its vein
lizards like a forties singer
gloved to the elbow
in lurex shine.

Theatrical legend,
fool's gold, dragon, fake:
its own membrane
rears an adamantine finger
to let lidless libido
pulse through its sunlit spine.

Inner note

Like a wishbone
or the instep of your foot

this parabolic love curves,
wings stirring

in the neck nerves of a crane
at marsh's edge,

or bends its back into a kite
arching the membrane of blue flight.

You breathe me out
I breathe you in

the smell of your skin
is salt and tide and tin.

The half-open door
tilts cooler light

upon the floor
and outside sounds come in,

an olive thrush
through the hibiscus bush

last evening note
throating me under you.

This much is all we have:
shadows gathering,

fugitive grace,
and the deep body as our penumbral space.

Stay here

for TM

Stay here, a little longer.
Stay here with me.

How easy it is for you to go,
step by step, print by print
as if you are just fetching
the washing off the line,
or stopping for the shopping
on your way from work,
just posting a subscription
for another year.

But ending up on another coast
where your dead are visiting overnight,
especially your wild friend
who wants you company so badly
he lies through his teeth,
promises if you stay night long,
there'll be wine, tobacco, debate,
and no women to call you back

importunately like this:
stay here a little longer, with me.

Tatamkhulu Afrika

To God

You are the stilled
fire at the heart of the glass,
the running fire of the wave,
the soundless conflagrations at the two
ends of the days, the glow-
worm's cold ember,
the least
rupturing of darkness into light,
blindness into sight,
knowing of the known
into knowing of the stone
heart of the stone.
Pinion me with the eagle
anger of Your Sight,
harass me with the blind
stubbornness of the mole
that paces me through the long
resonances of the soil,
ignite in me the white
Fury of Your Light,
torch the hollows of my bones,
melt from them my deviant flesh,
the wayward serpents of my blood,
for I come to You through many grades
of darkness, seeking Light,
seeking Love,
seeking that You splay
me for Your Rending, grant
me no peace, be
to me as the lean
and subtle leopard that,
by Your Grace,
is leopard,
and is Grace.
So, I, rent.

shall dare to hope to love
with something of Your Love,
to touch, to yield
to some other's touch,
with something of the quiet
Passion of Your Grace,
and be complete.

Dancing in my city

Preying mantis
of honed and naked power,
angling and clattering
round the cupping metal
of early spring's clear heaven:
but the lenses of its cameras
benign now,
poison-sacs retracted,
holding its own unholy holiday
in its own olympic otherness.

We watch it.
The mantis has been upon our backs before now:
we do not trust it,
feel still its skin—close hovering over us,
ratchet forelegs in the rib-cage,
hot breath of roaring motors.

We are on a peace march,
but still we flinch before the corners
for angles are for ambushes,
lateral precipices lurching
into cul-de-sacs of anguish.

Stomach-muscle-knotting
tongues of backward-rearing tissue caution
'stop here!',
but the feet move on, and the torso, trembling, follows,
shambling into yet another street of mellow
impossibly innocuous
sunlight.

Incredibly,
they have kept their promise:
they have left us
to dance, and sing, and flaunt our banners,
but my feet move heavily on the dull, blue tarmac:
I have been too long away from the once beloved city:
I am a stranger in the madam's bedchamber,
romping on a forbidden bed-cover,
black fingers, huge as spiders,
scuttling among the sacred toiletries.

Spectators, draping balconies,
are propped up, straw-stuffed effigies,
bead-button eyes alone alive and gleaming
with a mockery or a malice
that turns my spittle sour,
dries my rough, untutored, sweating blackskin,
slows me to the shy walk
of inept clown, throw-back
dompas-carrier.

But then I see her:
the little, yellow, dancing woman,
the rapt yet graven, shrivelled features,
generous San buttocks rolling
with a gentle, rhythmic, effortless abandon,
small feet skittering,
lightly as a water-bug on dust-glazed water,
along the crowd-crushed, dead macadam.

And my feet move on again, knowing
that under them,
lies still a soil forever Africa,
and it is not I that am the alien,
but they that stand here, streetside,
watching me
dancing in my city.

Maqabane

Like gnats after rain,
sudden beetles born
of thunder and storm,
we are the creatures of our time,
its passing wind,
murder done,
blood drying in the sun.
We drone,
not with the fat,
mellow hum of bees,
but the thin
snivelling of the fly;
or we roar, faces turned
to the never-listening sky,
cacophonous as ass or mule,
beaten till the dumb
tongue festers into sound.
We have no song?
How shall we sing?:
as they who, blind
to the blood on their shoes,
sing of lives that never come alive,
mimed and stilled as the moons
in the prisons of their nails,
thrushes in the hedges of their minds?
Does one scream
in careful cadences, stretched
upon a rack of pain,
measure metre when one tells
of the slit throat's roar,
ripped belly's gut spilt,
smoking, onto the cold tar,
charred body's settling
like the timber of a shack torched
by a midnight hand?
Beyond the darkness, grey
morning breaks: a bird,
or child,
uncertainly cries, our feet stir
a visible dust, we breathe

a freshening air.
The familiar is suddenly behind.
The grey men, the grey
singers of irrelevant song,
they who hid
behind the stillness of their hands,
slot into the patterns of our heels.
Maqabane – yes –
let us sound that sweet
endearment once
more before the dust
clogs our tongues –
they will have us now,
with the teeth of their laughter tear
the flesh from our bones,
crack them for the marrow they no longer hold.
It is the way.
But still,
within ourselves,
there is the secret hearth
of our love, the place
of the holding of our hands,
and if one harsh note
of our crying woke
a sleeping heart, steeled
a timid spine,
then we, too, sang,
scoring our songs in the flesh
of those that, dead, do not die.

The funeral of Anton Fransch

I went to Anton Fransch's funeral:
he held off the police for seven hours.

The minister
with careful logic sketched
a parable of ancient Babylon:
I savoured the aptness of the simile
but thought of Africa,

the photograph I had seen the night before:
a buffalo being dragged down by hyenas,
one eye ripped out, the bloodied muzzle
agape and bellowing.

Lately flushed
out of the closets of his ambivalence,
well-fleshed beneath the robes
of his unaccustomed Arabism,
the minor community leader droned
predictable pomposities,
eyes darting that way, this,
reminding me of the cockroach that,
when we had ripped up the floorboards of my tottering hovel,
had rushed about with kamikaze unstoppability,
seeking the sullen lair we,
and the sunlight,
had violated.

Only the advocate,
with customary shrewdness, traversed
a more accommodating territory,
not striving for the pinnacles of the professionals,
targeting not the dead son but the still living, disposable mother,
persuading from me one reluctant teardrop.

On the march,
we held the flag up with both our hands,
they having taken our staff for the great flag
roaring like a godswind about the fragments
of Anton Fransch in the box that held nothing but them,
only the voice living on, perhaps,
in a heart or the earth's groaning.

Four round housewives of Bonteheuwel
fled from the hot sun
into the flag's fluttering shadow,
using it as a sunshade,
shimmying and chattering only of that
which housewives customarily chat about,
gossiping over companionable fences.

We boarded the bus:
we were alone amongst children.
On the staircase behind me,
a boy and a girl touched,
slyly rather than shyly,
eyes rapacious rather than radiant
with the incontinent passion of their puberty.
The bus belched:
then moved and shuddered
to the pounding of fists, thudding of boots
of children grown suddenly, frighteningly ageless,
screaming obscenities at gathering squad-cars,
blue-bodied, imperviously watching
riot-squad policemen,
flags snapping and snarling, wind howling.
In the coffin,
the new, the sacred reliquary,
the handful of flesh and bone and sinew
that for seven improbable hours challenged
all the paraphernalia of power, shaming
them and us,
equally.

I went to Anton Fransch's funeral:
Did the tongues fall short because the tongue
cannot take the citadel?
Did the buses shudder
only with our hatred,
or the anguish also at our own inadequacy?
Did the four round housewives of Bonteheuwel
chatter only in their mindlessness,
or as birds do
when the serpent moves in the wasteland?

Anton Fransch was a very heavy hero:
I think, sometimes, we dropped him along the road somewhere,
and he lies there still,
in the seeding grasses,
the bright, blue moonlight,
and only the beetles, swarming,
bury him.

Hit squad

Suddenly, it's the way it was:
glowing green
of dashboard lights,
forward-leaning
shapes of heads,
smoke from cigarettes
snagging in my throat,
car radio playing soft,
shockingly inapt
lyrics about love.

Rocking strips
of lit streets slap
their tentacles of light
across my face;
spastic cries
of snatched-at crowds,
sibilances of other cars,
needle thin
silences we weave
about our fears.

Almost in each other's laps,
our closeness brings
no comfort, strength;
only shame
of the shapes we shield,
keeps us in our place,
permits
the odd rictus of a grin,
carefully weighed,
macho man's aside.

No Name
fidgets in the dark:
I sense the thin
phallus of the thing
I'll soon let spew
its flame.
My own loins ache

with the still held seed
of my lust to be
God's doomsday man.

We'll cross the street
in bright light,
aim high
to set the place,
not flesh, alight.
We're, after all,
honourable men,
regretting even
the burst window's
yawn of pain.

We'll leave to wail
of breached alarms,
first time terrified,
white screams,
squeal of wheels,
and No Name will loose
a small sigh of stress and look
with reverence at me
who am such a macho
leader of wild men.

We slow down:
it's so real, I reach
for what he holds, seize
a surprised hand;
it's empty save
for the tickets for the show:
most violent one this year, they say—
dead right, that,
for old lions denied
what old lions still need.

Nightrider

At the mountain's top, I reach up,
I fill my haversack with stars.
I am at the centre of the soundless night,
my bicycle's light alone still warms.
How wan that warmth,
how vast the cold that moves
through last year's long dead grass.
Always my dynamo's humming on the wheel
seems such a very winter sound.
Through many a long night it has followed me
up many a long hill, the white moonlight
spilling over us, white as the sea's foam.
Ah, that sea! roaring hugely
out of the huge night,
rearing on the black rocks below.
How tiny my cycle's light,
how minuscule my soul.

The fist

The poster's stone hand grips
the flag's staff:
straining knuckles thrust
against the skin.
There is nothing else:
no wrist, no arm.
Just a fist,
punching through my wall.
Grubby cellophane
tacks it there.
Why,
you ask,
the hand, why
not flowers, a bird,
stilled,
a sea's motionless rage?
Our spoor is not the same:
mine lies

on the shadow side of sand,
blood in it,
the beast's – or mine.
You graze on communal land
near easily accessible wells.
What do you,
the sea,
replicating waves,
bird going nowhere,
flower, headless, in a dead hand,
know of pain,
aloneness of the only living thing
threading in and out
of passing men,
touching them with hands
that hunger for a sign,
and there are none,
there are none?
Even the wall,
the back to it
sliming it with fear,
does not know
the ultimate aloneness of the night's
hammering on the door,
its flinging wide
to the blood and the rain.
But the fist knows,
and the dark,
savaged shape beyond knows,
driving the fist through the walls,
leaning on them till they crack
and the cracks leak
old litanies,
battle cries,
and the simulacra of dead
warriors seethe
through the hospices of my rooms.

The funeral

Her smile drains
between the pebbles of her teeth;
she hugs herself that her shiver may seem
but the cold running on her skin.
But her eyes betray
the tongue's casualness,
sham innocence
of her leaning to me to learn.
She drops back when I lift
the flap of the funeral tent,
pales when I look
into his face, wish well
the strange, still agonized
grimace of the dead.
I sense her flinch when I tell
of the tumult across,
about, the silent flesh,
the joyous levelling
of the living with the left:
the denial, even, of his death.
The gulf between us yawns
wider than the skylines of our worlds.
I try to understand her,
but she's cast
(as I am cast?)
in the granite of her shape:
stone ears hear
only the whisper of slow hymns,
decorous mourners' plodding steps,
solemn trundle of the hearse,
post-funeral's discreet
tinkle of teacups.
I talk and talk,
summoning rolling-buttocked mamas' dressed
in their Sunday best,
purple-yellow-red-
flowered cotton prints,
knotted doekies, bow
to the front, hiding heads
of stubble, plaits,
incipient dreadlocks.

Smiles as wide
as the widening of her eyes,
they fold me into their flesh,
welcoming me
to their celebration of a death.
Youth playfully jerks
my arm up behind my back,
meaning no disrespect,
not knowing his strength,
stiffens then, fist aloft,
in adulation of the dead,
head bent,
in smouldering, momentary grief.
Old Umkhonto we Sizwe friend,
posting the coffin's honour guard,
face fittingly stern,
movements marionette's,
winks in a huge
acknowledgement of me, not
undermining anything else.
Her hand's spiritlessness rejects
my taking it, her smile's
the dead's grimace.
Old woman, still
edgy as a cricket, links
her arm in mine, face clenched
inwards in the rapt
pleasure of the dance,
and we thunder up the road with the rest,
hustling the body to its long
reunion with its clay,
wearing away
of it by water and worm.
Her hand finds
its way out of mine,
pretending no intent.
I pretend it is I
that lets it go.
She sighs, turning her head aside.
I trace its line: white
sad trash, sad
deliberate fool?
Does she see

in me as cheap a trash,
no less a fool?
Wet multiple flesh,
sweat running like rain,
a sourness of dust, tang
of dung, of dark
cavities of the body that cry
for the least of life's
apportionment of grace,
rush me, trussed
in a new, yet old
as time, togetherness of skin,
to the grave's edge, ask
of heaven and earth,
of the fled soul,
the why of its going, stand
for a moment, soft
and reaching, child
wanting he should go easily down
the road we have walked with him a little way,
will in the end, too, walk all the way,
then bend to the burying,
clapping, shouting,
as the forbidden weapons splat
out their flat
salute and we turn
for the washing of the hands,
celebratory cracking of a coke,
taking up the baggage laid
for these few hours down.
I mumble death's
but the longer half of life,
explaining, ashamedly
seeking to be excused.
Her face is sheer:
I can hold
her silence in my hand
She says she will make tea.
I hear her in the kitchen:
shifting dress's
rustling like a dust,
tinklings of teacups,
shovellings of spoons.

Sleepless

Day's pain seeps
into the hollow of my back,
nests there,
aware, alert.
I cannot sleep.
If I lie on my side I might.
But it is not sleep I want.
I want hands that reach
deeper into me than my flesh,
my bone, my blood,
that find the breach the day has gapped
in the namelessness that knows
nothing, save
I am.
I need a healing of hands,
a priest
to exorcise a beast,
smash it through
the staring mirrors of my eyes.
There are flames on the walls.
I know there are cars out there,
flashing their lights:
but still the flames are on the walls.
I know the howling is the wind's,
that a glass dropped in the neighbouring house,
braai-fire's smoke beyond the fence,
late-night wanderer's random oath,
are just that, yet still I pace,
as one shaken from a sleep,
the thunderous square,
doomsday acreage of my soul,
see, hear, smell,
these same things, reach
out in terror, caught
up in the cataracts of the backs,
long scream
of midnight's hurtling train,
faces, known,
unknown, flickering past,
buds of eyes
bursting open with the blind,

cold fire of the stars.
Under the sheet,
my hand clasps
a stone, I smash
a window, set
a car alight,
trapped raven of my throat caws
in exultation, weeps
at the hating of my heart.
I scream
defiance at the watchers, wink
away tear gas, draw
love that is strength from sweat-
slicked companionable flesh,
slap a white-
faced woman caught
in an angle of a wall,
turn away, remembering her eyes,
shaking hands shielding her breasts.
In a small silence, the wind
comes to me,
kisses me on the mouth,
strokes my cheeks.
I drink
its sweetness as one
who thirsts before a death.
New fleeing brings
me to my knees, a face
dissolves, a hand
that held a stone lies spread
in the innocence of a leaf.
Pain in my back stirs:
or is it the beast,
moving in my belly, its slime
slick between my thighs?
Is there no holy man,
sunken in his prayers,
shriven as I am not,
who will come to me like the wind,
lay on me the saintliness of his hands?
Till then,
how shall I sleep?

Queue

They pass me,
hurrying in the shared rain,
drenched bodies bent
forward into the wind.
Their odours stay with me,
ripe as spring cats',
as lovers' sheddings on a skin.
Others wore
what they now wear:
nothing fits.
Too short pants
show hopelessness of tattered socks;
T-shirts ruck
up over spines,
bare buttock-clefts;
shoes squelch,
shapelessly,
in standing rain.
They will not have eaten yet:
hunger small cat
clawed into the belly's side.
It is nothing new:
pre-dawn Khayelitsha train
is for men that strap
their bellies with broad belts,
hold them when they howl.
Swinging slack-
limbed down the street, they pass
girl outside the takeaways.
Bathed in green
saturnalian neon-glow,
she bites into the pie's
soft crust, finds
their eyes fixed on her,
turns, hastily, away.
In unison as birds
in flight, they swerve
suddenly aside.
I am alone in the rain.
Block along, I find

them in a queue in a lane.
Sign on a gate says:
'Labourers apply'.
They jostle, shift
their feet,
peer around the backs ahead:
eager to know more,
feverish with the life of the lean,
the fire that feeds on bone.
I hear a soft skirl
of slogans in my mind.
They're still there,
hours on;
still crouched to catch
the suddenly flung bone.
Yet it is not the same:
woebegone, round eyes stare
no further than their shoes,
flanks quiver like struck hounds'.
Somewhere the sun's
riding high
in an Indian summer sky:
but here the rain spills, ceaselessly, down,
wells from every seam.
Thin fingers thrust
into pants' long pockets, chase
last coins,
count them where they lie:
the queue has eyes.
They're thinking of home,
door snatched inwards as they near,
dragging on its hinge,
darknesses like bedded kine
rising with soft cries,
unbearable expectations of eyes.
Knife-blade-bright
water in a pot
waits to dance, to sing,
to hold a festival.
I feel my body sag
with the emptiness of their hands.

Respite

Yesterday a cloud burst.
They say trees were blown down,
and a dog died.
I got home chicken-wet.
This morning a wedge
of pigeons sliced
across a clean sky,
and the moon,
shaving off it, lazed
down onto Lion's Head.
Succulent, thick
dock-leaves spread
their salad greens,
suckled the sloshed earth;
and sudden, frail
filigrees of vines,
luminous and pale as spiders flushed
from under a too-long-bedded stone,
wove and stretched their grace across
the for once forgotten ruins,
I beguiled
by the delilah green,
wind-after-the-rain's
sly cossetting of my skin.
I tried to grow a shame:
but it would not take.
Anointed with a holy oil of joy,
swept along on starlings' song,
I hit town.
'Come to the Rally' yellow posters slapped
their silly sides
all the way down Sir Lowry Road,
and even the man from Khayelitsha
nearly smiled.
So the morning spun
for me its long lie,
led me on the leash of gold
it threaded through my nose,
was about me
with a sound of bells,

played the wanton with my old bones.
Now the sun's barbarous gong
booms down into the quavering sea,
bloodying its waves,
and I feel the wind, boding rain,
veering northwest again,
and the blade I danced so deftly on
is cutting through me into pain.

The accident

There is no mistaking it:
that dull, sodden thump
of a man struck down.
His bruising is a bruising
of all flesh, cracked bones'
inward, resonating pain.
The car throbs over him,
black tyres pads
of a creature stopped
in mid-stride, front fenders
glittering in a slash
of brilliant, bared chrome.
Headlamps island him
in light, torn clothing flaps
like a moth with broken wings caught
in the black,
silent torrent of the street.
He is lying on his back,
leg angled under him,
arm flung wide,
red silk mask of his blood lending
blessed anonymity to his face.
Flittering in and out
of the circle of the light,
the driver is bellicose,
explanatory, profane,
suddenly, impossibly, revolving around
the rolled-in-its-rags,
blood-and-alcohol-redolent

ruin of a man.
People are gathering,
seeping silently in
from the alleys and lanes.
Bodies fret
around me in jeans,
T-shirts, whores' clinging sheaths.
The air is thick
with the soft, boiling-out-of-holes
serpentine-sibilance
of flesh and clothes,
slavering, tense,
baying-for-blood breath
of ancient
snout-to-the-moon-man.
Caught up,
helplessly as a sea-tumbled shell,
in the slow,
tidal suck of the crowd,
I sway
in unwilling unison,
share its mute,
mindless dropping of the jaw,
take from it the stagnancy
of wine-soured flesh,
dagga-zoll's bitter-sweet tang.
He is one of us;
yet we look at him
with insectile, uncaring eyes,
and the night is a lamentation
in a skewed,
johnny-come-lately liberated land,
till she, white,
the driver's wife,
kneels down with a tissue,
wipes the face clean,
and we see
he has been crying, silently, all this time,
and someone spreads a coat over him
that has many patches,
and someone goes to the telephone.

Glimpse of God

There's such a stillness, Lord,
I hardly dare to breathe,
must scrupulously place
my foot, my hand, for fear
they quake a world not meant for men,
breath rend
a heaven a glass
spider has spun.
Each leaf's
trembling's like a hair
a terror's raised,
yet here
is no terror, Lord,
but the electricity of love:
Yours as theirs.
Impelled
a petal tilts
to the imminent sun,
to Your Light beyond light that yet
is never gone,
and almost it seems I feel
the far waves fold
in a froth-of-gold,
fan
in an ocean-vast
surrender on the sand.
Somewhere a small
bird's leaking a small song,
liquid as water in a wet shade,
and I'm one
with it in Oneness though,
soon now,
the city will wake and You
again be but the Silence on
the high hill's stone.

Karen Press

This is not a riot policeman

Look:
three sweet blue riot policemen
standing watching the goldfish in the Gardens
somebody loves these bastards
somebody takes the wicked blue cap off at night
and strokes the poisonous brow

how they must hate
something, to beat and beat
at women's breasts and the heads of children
until they bleed and crack

with their sharp moustaches
and their smooth, fat cheeks
they're worth every pound of meat
their mothers feed them

fat, furious riot policemen
watching the goldfish in the Gardens

She brought home poppies

she brought home poppies
instead of bread, twelve little suns

the eldest child asked why? why poppies,
buying poppies when there is no food?

she said, look at them, who can be hungry with these
yellow, white, orange suns facing every corner

all night they rustled on their long stems
as if the room were a forest

and the children crying,
she made them into birds in the forest

in the morning the petals had fallen,
pollen dusting the floor, the youngest asked

what will we eat today? collecting the petals
she stored them away carefully

Bird

bird
and shadow of bird
shadow and shadow and shadow of bird
drifting over the sea's eyes
tired over the eyes of winter

bird raining
feathers stoning the sea
bird wing beating hard hard
bird heart stoning the sea
the sea the sea the calling come home sea
deep voice of the dark water

cave of the sea
bird voice rising
cave of the sea, water cave rising
and shadow of bird
sea shadow of bird

Hope for refugees

you can go back
you can go back
run backwards
call back the cattle
unstitch the hems
pull the photos out of the fire

you can go back
you can go back
pull down your dress
button your shirt
wipe off the blood
scrub off the blood

you can go back
you can go back
wash the walls
fix the door
remember the step down in the dark
avoid the dark

you can go back
you can go back
dig up the box in the front garden
dig up the box in the yard
dig up the box in your heart
dig up the box in the child's heart

you can go back
you can go back
lay out the skeletons in their beds
hang out the years to air
plant seeds, keep watch at the well
tear up your nightmares, your footprints
lock the door
work hard
give thanks to god

from *Tiresias in the city of heroes*

Tiresias remembers

A man came, unfortunate bridge. Tiresias:
with his dangerous memory come to the city of heroes.
Foolish man, looking for a woman
to watch her say again, go away.
Melting memories into dreams with a blind longing,
the hot longing that opens darkness,
melting the dreams of heroes into memories,
aching, aching.

*

A man arriving is an emissary or an enemy.
Tiresias holds his poor broken heart under the shedding jacaranda
as the heroes undo him with questions.

'Tell us the story of the war we won.'
Like children looking for a history to wear.

What do I remember? Standing in the sun for hours listening to
speeches while my feet burned on the ground. Walking along
streets where women stood at every door crying. Hacked
bodies. A little man who followed me for three kilometres and
when I finally tried to grab him he begged me to teach him to
sing, but I thought he was lying and killed him. A baby with its
stomach carved out and a policeman standing next to it,
vomiting. Being given a computer and told to write. The smell of
beer on dead men's lips. Sitting in a shebeen drinking brandy
after brandy and getting so happy I felt like flying. A woman
laughing as another woman's house burned down. Yellow cars
and vans: that thick flat yellow like sweet icing on a cake. The
noise of helicopters. My mother saying don't go, or don't come
back. My child screaming when I tried to pick him up. Meat
roasting at my child's funeral. A book with my photo in it.
Crowds becoming silent. A man who shot his wife in a meeting.
The noise of helicopters. My burning feet. Bodies in the street
covered in blankets.
My home is a place I'm frightened of. It's a big sore inside me
that burns when I touch it.

'Are you not bigger than your own backyard?
In that war each of us became the nation:
the whole nation entered into each of us.
Tell us that story.'

That story. That story:
In Sharpeville your arms died.
In Uitenhage your tongues died.
In Boipatong your eyes died.
In Katlehong and Bekkersdal and Empangeni you died and
                                    you died and you died.
That's what I remember.

In Pretoria your fingernails became joint chief of staff.
In Pretoria your teeth ran the central bank.
In Pretoria your hair was the president.
That's what I remember.

In Jo'burg your heart was tortured and died.
In Cape Town your skin joined the enemy police.
In the veld and the mountains your memory buried its children.
That's what I remember.

That's what I remember.
All this dead and defeated, is your story.
Only the hair and the shadow still growing,
responding to sunlight, and I ask myself
which body were they grafted onto, in that moment of darkness
before total victory was declared?
My home is a place I'm frightened of.

The heroes leave him in the marketplace
like an old newspaper, blurred with the truth,
sifting the dry breeze for her scent.

                        *

In a cool room she lies on the mourning mat.
Themba, he says, Themba, Themba.
You are still here.

You are still here, she says with the voice of dead bullets.
He is gone and you are still here.
Why couldn't they kill you?

*

There's nothing to remember.
What remains is here.
Its origins will repeat themselves.
How this man got his power
and that man starves
will not glue joy to your heart.
Sing or dream
or keep silent inside your bandages.
Don't dig, it only cuts the roots
and whatever is growing now will wither
like what came before.
Silence is big enough to hold the present
wide open for you to breathe in.

Heart's hunger

I

I stored you against my eyelids
my treasure, more precious than water.

> *Then they stole my home, my land,*
> *the possibility of my hands, my last dress.*

I saw them, and when my eyes closed
I could not remember you.

> *Hunger has eaten my dreams.*
> *You are a scarecrow in a field*
> *the birds have plundered – useless love.*
> *Send money; I cannot eat your pink words.*

The moon will not believe me.
She says my hart is beating in your vanished hands.

II

This woman walking along the road
keeps seeing her heart fall behind her
bleeding into the buried caul.

This woman walking along the road keeps walking.

Her heart keeps falling away from her.

She roasts the falling heart on tinder fires
to sell to hungry travellers.

She dreams of arms wrapped around arms.

She dreams she is a feather on a flying bird.

She dreams of an enormous mother beckoning her.

She carries her father on her journey's back.

Her stomach is filled with his bones.

She burst with pain and continues walking.

Her heart drops away, drops away.

She calls 'I love you' in the wind.

The words hang like dead birds around her ears.

She is a stick no-one will hold.

      Far away, her name has faded on a man's dry skin.

She lies down on the gravel.

A thorn tree grows through her,
pushing her upright.

III

The woman with the thorn tree growing through her chest
                                        arrives in the city.
She sees a picture of a house with grass and water,
and a doorway in which people embrace.
She decides to become such a house.

She sits on the sandy floor of the city.

She plucks an orange from the gutter and sells it to a hungry man.

> A man grabs the orange and eats it fast,
> thinking the taste of the woman seller.
> It wasn't enough.

She has six cents in her hand, she shows it to the moon.

IV

> *The moon curses me, turning away*
> *and I juggle with oranges in the dirt.*
> *I juggle with coins I plaster my skin with hands.*
> *The moon curses me, returning.*
>
> *Everyone is hungry, every mouth eats me.*
> *I am only so many crumbs of air, a sky*
> *covered with ants, they carry me piece by piece away.*
> *The moon stays, stroking the black bone beneath.*
>
> *What if I had waited for him on the road? .*
> *Moon, you know nothing.*
> *My hands held no offering for him.*
> *I am cursed with myself.*

V

Trader in hungers,
she grew strong.

And everything that could be eaten, was eaten.

She was bricks, words, skin, bread.

She was fire, milk, the road, the shade.

Her roof stretched wide across the city.

In her doorway people embraced.

The moon grew thinner and thinner
watching over the wastelands of her abundance.

VI

Ghost against trees, lucent hunger
or thirst? Is it silver water
that would bring you back to me?

I am dry sticks, my love,
and I hunger so for the greenness
of hands on me, I am the carcass of dreams,
you may drift through my spaces.

Where do you sleep,
who do you love,
are you somewhere else a man?
Transparent love, your body
holds my earth and sky,
you are the window open on my drought.

You are a dead ghost.
I am rich and you will eat none of my coins.
You are a memory ghost.
Nothing is promised me.
From hunger to wealth I have come
through the desert of my heart.

The man with incomplete words on his roof

The man with incomplete words on his roof
haunts the streets in search of additional letters.

Old green letters
and spaces.
His sheet of tin has old green letters and spaces
spread across it.

Someone looking down at the roof
would make no sense of it.

He hunts for more letters that green, that old.
He steals lettered tin
from other people's roofs and walls
trying to find the match.

People wake up with a dog staring at them from the yard
or rain in their hair.
They chase him, they take back their sheets of tin.
Cursing his incomplete roof
they tell him to throw it away, they offer
to buy him a new sheet of tin, plain silver.

No, no.
He wakes each morning from a dream
that the letters have washed away. Sweating, he climbs up
to find them.

His neighbours watch him from their rooms
with missing walls. They talk
of painting over the letters with black paint.

Sometimes they find the sounds of the spaces in their throats.

I who live here, it is I

'This earth was the first to speak,
I have been pronounced once and for all.'
– Breyten Breytenbach, *Return to Paradise*

I

In my sleep I return here.

*

Being here, giving birth to my city I am
day by day being home, day by day
it has no name, seeds came from all parts of the known world
to plant me here, being myself these rooms, streets, rain, tides,
the air tasting of me, cool mist my hair, my skin hot stone,
the pulsing of hands my hands growing sand and wood
as the sky enters my eyes and the sea wells from my feet
and I turning inside out disappear into all manner of joyous
                                                      bird cries
and the weeping of engines and wind,
gulls and avid rats feed where I feed,
consuming this limitless home swelling inside me
as I inside it open wide enough to die.

*

Coming home I see it coming towards me,
rubbing against me like a welcoming cat.

In my sleep I feel it leaning against me, sleeping.

*

Dried apricots, soft and sour
dawn wind stings the palm tree.

Neon rivers spilling across
the smell of buses pushing homeward.

*

In my sleep I return here.

II

It is only one look, one acrid glance shearing across the sweet
blue hour
and the air pulls back, embarrassed at its intimacy,
leaving me naked as a captured slave, a trespasser, a thief.

All people ask: what are you doing here? what are you?
Eyes and eyes and eyes, scraping my shadow off all surfaces.

Any person here rebukes me.
Any person here in the streets of my home rebukes me.
I, walking like a strange person in the streets of my home
stare at my footsteps spread out on the road and deny them.
Any person is more at home here than I am.

The walls and the wind withdraw obediently from my skin.
I breathe in the bitter juice of any person looking at me,
peeling me off the air, expelling me.

All people live in my home and say it is not me, it is not,
all people invite me in and say look, it is not yours, welcome.

Any person has permission because of history.
Because of justice. Because of songs of genesis.
Any person being decidedly here in my self
banishes me. Any person refuses permission.
Any person who says nothing, or everything,
does not say my name. Any person is here in my place,
it is not my place.

How is it that my born home
is loyal to anyone who passes
in the street, following him like a hot beast
eager for better origins?

III

They say if my name were found here
buried in rock older and older
than any home a person can recall,
my home would return to me.

But no name is my home.
I am spread wider over the sand
than the width of a name.
Being born here the cells of my skin
are all the time of history.

What voice could pronounce the whole tide of my days?
What eyes could pour sky into my sky?

If this could be, if anyone here
were here with me inside the water and the wind
my home would flow through me and through anyone
and return to me, return to me in my sleep.

Humus

Without words or plans I was arriving
led by the surf, the days, the small streets and balconies,
worms and beetles came to fetch me,
by the waters of my homeless years I lay down gratefully,
ocean salts drifted in over my lips,
my eyelashes left like yachts on a further journey

I lay down, settling
so deep down, crumbling like bread
or the source of roses, honey, eggs

One by one my cells set out through tiny mouths,
atoms I knew moved along twigs, perched
on the tip of a thorn over some bird's wing feathers,
close enough to smell its arrival

Curiously my genes made proposals:
now the dune grass sings in a familiar voice,
a bed of succulents has grown pale and thoughtful,
the parapet of a building flicks its hair in the sun

All the while I lie here inside the seasons
watching the endless generosity of my bones,
mornings and planets keep coming to fetch me

Dispossessed words
found poem

for Jessie Tamboer, who set herself alight and burned to death because she
could no longer provide food for her children

Trucks carried 40 000 blacks to the southern edge of the desert.
I cannot say anything about my future now.
              We had a very beautiful view
                and this was the first time I saw my father cry.

They said 'Old man, are you moving?'
I took a crowbar, pulled the house down.
I cannot say anything about my future now.

                              *

              A man must have a dumping ground.
              Every rabbit has got a warren.
              A native must have a warren too.

                              *

Sometimes I cry, I
the absolute poor
I am sick to death of watching my ruin.

                              *

We had a very beautiful view of the sea –
              This was refused.

                              *

Uncovering rubbish bins, I ask, could it not be that something
                              has been thrown in here –
just a little something that I can chew?

This was refused.

                              *

At times she would just suddenly start sobbing without any
                              apparent reason.

The absence of love.
There is no way you can describe that hunger.
Shining clean pots and jars:
There was no food whatsoever in the house.

*

She was immediately engulfed by flames but did not utter a
               sound as she walked around the yard burning.

The ashes of one household are collected by another for the
                         bits of coal.

If you want to survive you must make a plan.

I cannot say anything about my future now.

*

Reclaiming our land

Every map is out of date.
The roads go to unbuilt houses.
How do the tortoises know
there's bush on the far side of the tar?

At night stars fall like gooseberries,
one into my lap, one into your lap,
husked in cosmic permissions.
Everyone gets a star.
Soon there'll be none left.
You have to eat it; they aren't for planting.

Put up a mirror where you are
and make yourself at home in your familiar eyes.
Outside the wind blew it all away.

Welcome

soldiers and stockbrokers
shake hands:
there are no sides any more

bananas are growing on the pear tree
Pik's moustache extends and curls
a satisfied cat flicks its tail
in the cream
                    three black hairs float there

volcanic sunsets bleed over toasting lovers
the ice-cream man collects unused condoms
the cars drive straight upward
on the mountain sliding into the sea
the speaking totem pole in the sky
is called Nelson

bananas are growing on the pear tree
a yellow bag full of pink notes
sails down the cableway
little hands open and close like venus flytraps
black ones

there's snow everywhere
the roads are melting
welcome home, exiles and entertainers
you get three shares in a pear tree
a bullet and a banana
to help you settle in: shake hands

Statues

Some lonely men stand around this city
petrified in difficult moments.

They have the eyes of people who never felt love,
so alone, achieving the country.

The people they achieved never notice them,
the contradictory pulling of muscles inside the metal.

Like stray outcropping of rock.
It's impossible to believe they were ever the cause of anything.

This, too

The child's fingers breaking the wings at the joint
thrill with the feathery heat of the bird's pain.

Pushing the axe through bone, amazed
a man sees his hands glow with the life running into them.

This woman cuts her flesh with steel and lies back
watching her mysterious red agony escape.

Who placed shackles on the human repertoire?
Killing gives pleasure, dying is half our skill.
This we can do, with voice and heart and will.

Causality and chance in love

Chapter 1

His parents
and my parents
caused it all.

That's not true. God, laughing as he turned the page.

Two atoms coughed out
by time's collapsing star.

Libra ascending straight into Scorpio
through Sharpeville, Robben Island and Mowbray.
Arriving in Sea Point
when the law was repealed.

Now we are possible.
Necessary and sufficient conditions.

This happy world that fills our arms.

Chapter 2

Robben Island was more useful
than the little Swiss chalet
with the man and the lady
swinging in and out unreliably
or stuck; the mercury still as a dead ant.

IF YOU SEE	IT WILL BE
the clear outline of the island	rain is on the way, and winter winds
a smudge of land in a brown haze	there is dangerous smog in the air
a shimmering blue blur	there will be long and windless heat

*'The healthy colony of penguins
is Robben Island's pride and joy.'*

'I remember the first time all of us heard children's voices in the
quarry. It was as though we had suddenly been struck by
lightning. We all stood dead still, and every one of us was
waiting for the moment when we would glimpse that child. And
of course it wasn't allowed. The warders quickly went and made
sure that we didn't actually see the kids. Just those lone voices –
the one occasion in ten years that I actually heard the voice of a
child.'

Chapter 3

Mist rising on the winter waves
swathed your quarried words in veils
and blew them in to fill my chest with sleeplessness.

I watched the kelp arms of sea creatures reaching
through the swell.
You caught the glint of closed windows on the sunlit hills.

Only the wind passing across your lips

and then across my lips, preoccupied with its cargo of rain,
could have imagined us both in the same breath.

Chapter 4

We two waltzing strangely across sand bearing us
tideward, looking over each other's shoulders

at our futures, their lightless eternities
radiating power. Space is curved. We will meet each other

again and again in our pasts that call themselves home,
a little distance from the sunset come to fetch us.

This laughing history that fills our arms.

Ancestors

Clues

1.   Outside it snows
        and horsemen ride in with guns.
        An old man in a prayer shawl
        sips tea through a sugar cube.

        If he had looked up
        he would have seen through the doorway
        a small child standing in sunlight far away
        waving to him: he might have waved back.

2.   Women laughing in a hot kitchen
        unto the last generation.

3.   On a train someone sits, weeping,
        eating the last bread from her mother's hand.

4.   They looked back from the deck of a ship
        at the quay. Strangers watched them go.

They remember only their own voices.
Here are no graves to visit.

5.   Two lit candles.
        Gold words embroidered on blue velvet.
        Sweet wine.

6.   Grodno, 1850.
        Khar'kov, 1990.

7.   Shepherd over bare rock.
        Cloth merchants.
        Owners of books.
        Men who wore waistcoats.
        Women who died young.

8.   The wheatear and the tern go back.
        They return without messages.

9.   The child holds a cobweb of old wedding lace
        and a small string of grey pearls.

        She places her ear against sepia lips, waiting.

The first thirty-seven years

We were just camping out.
I put up a wall
and my mother bought carpets.
There was a door for the sea.

My father stood dropping anchor
year by year. I watched him lowering the rope,
he was swaying with a faraway look
and he said he loved me, lowering the rope.

My brother kicked a ball around a lot
and I was reading. I never knew
he broke his heart young.
I buried mine in a wave.

My father died. My mother went home.
My brother was away somewhere, walking.
I moved to the other side of the wall,
just camping out.

The sea could come in my sleep, or the wind.
I've no rope, my father left no rope.

Rotten fish

Law and order isn't easy.
Anyone can lay a charge.
The door of the police station is always open.

Sergeant Oliphant (unaware
he's descended from a long line of Ndlovus
with other, ongoing concerns)
has no reason to believe he should believe
a woman who smells and drips sand,
accusing unknown people of murdering
other unknown people.

He scratches his head.
'Salt water cures lice,' Alida says.

Anyone is capable, Sergeant Ndlovu tells himself.
Shall I arrest every person on the beach
who has refused this woman something?
Murder is a cloudy thought.

Sergeant Oliphant would like very much
not to make a dangerous mistake.
He knows that law and order
is just a thin umbrella carried by those who pour the rain.

'Get out of here,' he says.
'You smell like rotten fish.'

Seitlhamo Motsapi

shak-shak

& the carnival entered the last streets
    of the shantytown of

    my soul//lightning speed rhythm
light moving heavy swinging hip

& so the poor wd throw pots of paint
curdled in the heart to the drowsy skies

so the portraits wd sprout, paint
of our joy colouring the clouds

riotous multicolour, righteous marching
shak-shak prophet majaja in front

riotous bell & thundering drum
shak-shak mthembu foot

sore from his impatient corns

& the carnival entered the last street
    shack shack landscape grey

hunger a mere sunshine away/& yet
& yet the joy—profuse like air

mirth in madness, spirits rejoicing

& so the madmen—the high
voltage jolly demons, feet

shoo shoo shifty snap shuffle

& so the merry madmen of my soul

had the season's last stomp
after the chafe & bruise
of the 8 to 5 tortures

& while the electrick carnival
    kicked the weals off
    for the redeemer

already there's a sign
in the sky
for those who see

already the graffiti's up
the walls of my soul:

HISTRYS ON DE SIDE
OF DE OPRES

samaki

for water
water & the things
of water
holler us welcome

welcome to bird's vocabulary
scrawled across skies
welcome to lily's vernacular
sprawled across the parch
welcome to the fish's multiple infinitude
welcome to the desert's insistence
welcome to the jagged margin
where songs splinter inwards
while my talkative mirrors
flower into foam

the king of water
hollers us welcome

there are no spirit leftovers here

there are no fretting incompletions here
there are no lost pilgrims here
there are no amputated hand
    shakes here no
    quakes running out of the bone

i brother the flock & pasture
i gather the flocking posture
of the inner supple
i am every wound's rainbow
i am every manacle's forgetfulness
i am every knife's prostration

beyond the pikin gesture
their cars are dancing
into sulphurous convulsions
beyond bread & baptisms
they uncurl their greed

for us
water's brotherness
hallelujahs us welcome

djeni

1—calabaas

i am the new man
tall & cool
calm like a spear
tall like the sun—
    seh the assnologists
    lush & redded in the micro/scopegoat
      of tyori

i am the new man
   cool & connected
   bones blk & rotting to riddim
   obeah they lacktrick me a jig
     jungle jingle me kush/in meroe
       or eden

i am the nude mad
   drums warring blur in the head
   loinskin mosguito google
     friendli & fissical—
       seh the amfropologists

i am the nu man, mad i chant
   love song—bobbledigoon i mumble
chant me michael jerksin the spepi s/perm
while they kwashiorkor me
   they the world
   as sah geldof shuttles out
   of the sand of the tv crew
   in addis

2—bamako

O Lahd
is this my people so
this writhe in my I
a reed so green machete is greed
a sun a boulder for clouds to perch
is this mah people so
a weal on the kiss/a bleed inside
fire eating the bridge ash in the granary
the long knife of traitors cosy in the song
i remember rains harvest feast God in the hut
when love was the sky
& remembered the fields with the first rains
when hope was a sprout
a fire that showed promise
—wd spread far & high, the elders sd

i return to you now
as the hills refuse to sing
love was here, they seh
but for me there is only
the sure thud of a slow maul
only the bleeding slit
from the razor lips of snakes
a pat on the back that is not pat

i ask for bread
my brother feeds me stone
i ask for the green sha/door of his hand
he mumbles dollar blood

see this dear Lawd
the arrogant thunder
that runs into my heart
love in the mud
a rend in the sky

3—dhiki

ninety two afiriki
sun is not sun anymore
song is not salt nor crop
joy is not calabash
yam is a fading memory
herds slink into ash
while the quick axe or ache
of politricking spiders
rags hope to a distant flutter
the languid mumble of healers
comes to rest in the sky
feet fall into the long straggle
of weary nomads
home is the tarpaulin swamp
where the razor harmattan is home
hope is the hungry gruel
at the glutted feet of the world
that remembers me only
in the clustered fly of the tv crew
afiriki ninety two
song is song no more
but the long bleat of ends

ityopia phase-in

'we have only come for the sphinx we do not desire war'

1   prolude-Makuria

we bring news
from a far country
we bring you news
from your forgotten brethren

the sun eats into the marrow
of the manyatta
         they say
ever so slowly water recedes
from the wells
& soon no more dung
from the straggling camels
for our huts

it all starts
with the proselytising hordes
crescent dawns riding blood
into the village
as salaam asphyxiated the shrines
of our mud & copper defences

it all starts
on the anxious red wave
of the hell/meted mishinari
who saw other purposes
for my woman
beside pounding yam

it all starts
with babu acompong
who clanked mah village into dungeon
for a rusted musket

& didn't hear
the venomous viper hiss
that only came to bleed the lands

into a backward crevice
into malarial swamp
feeding theses
of rinsing anthro   pol   ogists
from oxbridge or makerere

now our suns have shrunk
& the horizon twigs
into the arid waistline
of the sahara

& while my three piece straightjacketed son
jives his ancestral integrity
for more cowries at the imf
i ride the 5 to 9 matatu
into bwana's sprawling fart

2   asante se dusk

so songhay fell

mali timbuctu ghana
the constellation of mossi

before you cd say Onyame
the invading dust
of the arab hordes
had overwhelmed the land
the clamorous rabble
of our cities of stone
melting into a whimper
beneath the urgent hoofs
of moor & mulatto

of sankore
all that remains
is the jagged scrawl of thin memories
a precarious groove in the shifting sands
of distant pasts

whether nkrabea or njia
only the red in the niger can tell
the despair of mansa musa's steel
clanking against the approaching dusk
ravenous voids taking over
whole empires

3   makorokoto

we salute you
al jahiz
  the prophet has returned
  peace & the first rains be upon him

so the barbarians in basra
in their boiling fervour
cd not subdue the pra-pra spue
of your trumpet over the hudson
across the limpopo
& the bleeding hell of their white crocodiles
beyond the thames & her fanged filth
of colonial afterdreams

the village soothsayer remembers
the melted soft staccato
of your advancing truths
despite the sugared skew
of apostate & infidel
the skies could not ignore you

see now what armies whirl the horizons
into hasty embraces

& the poor suddenly remember
the sanctuary of the rock
refuge in the machete
a rebirth in the scythe

brotha saul

dear ras

    i greet de lyaans
    in their roar of marble
    frozen in their gloss of postcard

    i greet u lyaan
    in yr mane of fire
    yr den of selassie
    yr glut of slave flesh

    what a boom of exploding riff
    what a tremor of bassline
    thunder of drum
    yr rock of voice
    whatta bomb-bomb
    yr stained finger of kaya
    calling from mount zion

lissen ras lissen here
jus don let de green of de spliff
curtain u from the red of mah blood
a piggin babylon runs with de gold

don let de rhythm ride u
when mah glass of freedom splinters
don let u be muted rub-a-dub
to de clang-a-lang-lang of de chain
as mah green of tomorrow
gives in at de knee

lissen ras
i write u so short
as outside fire mounts up de road
des a firebomb shattering
brotha's skull goes a-cracking
while de blinking on/off blue light
& de noising pierce of siren scream
confuse de night

remember lyaan
death hovers above like ready vultures
    mah bass is de fire
    blood muffles de drum
    & de mic gurgles red

i'll keep u de yelling red
while i chase de looted gold
mah green is a bridge to u

till then
    ras
        keep de lyaans roaring
        xex

missa joe

all jegged & tie
he forgets smiles & rivers
he forgets the ancient sugar of handshake
while his name slumps into sneer snarl
monosyllabic fester cripple
or dragon snore gripple

i offer him
the deep dizzying water of respects
from the hills & the herds
but he barks into the weary puddle
of offich inglish & boss shittish

so now
the purple of his rubber stabs
grows into a wall
but the drums won't fall asleep
    the drums won't fall asleep

andif

it is that time
it is that time love
the moon finally speaks with her six tongues
the rivers now forget the ocean
the mountain finally spits us out
from her centuries old sanctuary

it's the time of traitors
hasty like alligators in search of graves
it's the time of the long machete
arrogant like storms that blow into hearts
it's the time of nights
clamorous like abysses where death rests
it's that time my love
the mountain floods us her angry weals
that bruise screams into whimpers

i want you only to remember
the lacerated earth that bleeds into your feet
i want you only to remember
the past that screams at us
from the rent bellies of weary skies
the multiple incisions of dead loves
hurry our hearts into skewed postures

tomorrow there'll be no chain or chafe
no bleed or slit—no gash or ash
to whirl us into genocidal frenzies
there'll be no coffins with incomplete crosses
for men who died without crowns or rainbows
there'll be no knee dancing into a bruise

the lungs of dungeons will suddenly burst
into breezes that remember our wounds

there'll be only you & me
& vengeant warriors with spears knotted
into rainbows
there'll be me & you only
& our hearts mad with insistent loves

that demand mountains & skies
    skies & suns!
    the ancient composure of the hills!
    the roar of rains for all of us!
    the obstinate roar rage of the ocean
    for all of us!
    the eternal holler of hope
    for all of us!

the sprout of dreams & hymns
    for all of us

without delay!

brotha saul
    (furtha meditashuns)

dear ras
    is me pleasure
    to have pen on paper again
    —about the few shells of heart
    that remain
    when all is splinter & wreck
    rubble sore souls & rot is all

    we have the sun
    we have the moons
    seas of flower & her riots
    of rainbow colour

    we have the lead too
    & her clamorous staccato
    of bleeding ends
        whole
      pyramids of
    horizontal mortality
    fleets of wood & eternal rest
    scrounging downwards for
    the frozen embrace of clod & root

ras tell me why it so
why the blood keep calling
& only u & me always
running for cover
& our pigging friend
can't even remember
can't remember the stolen pasture
can't even remember
   fire of spear from the hills
can't even remember
his bleeding rivers of
non-retiefiable thievings of land

shadows take over the land
& dead worms bleed us to peace

i send u the first rains ras
   seas of harvest
      till i hear from u
         xex
          (of this world)

kulu

so the mesenja arrived
dust on his feet the silent speak
of the wearied creep of genial distances

before he even spoke
     —a roar rant to rubbery whisper
     in the climb & fall of griot's lilt
there was a slow swirl of hopes
the thud or thunder of tomorrow's suns
swelling a green scent in the air

     it will rain
     it will rain
     only set yr hearts right

     it will rain, it will rain
     though yr dances were a bruise
     & yr love didn't know breezes

enia

my love is like a river or a fist with forty fingers
my love is like a river that swallows mirrors & saxophones
& spits out the purple pink salt of songs without heads
while the skies dance like loa grandmothers

my love is a forty headed fist
sated on the scented innards of mediocrities
that smile like overdressed rainbows
while temples run into my frenzied wounds
my love is like a road that has grown wings
travellers drum their contemptible corrosions
up the walls of my head
that spits out the tasteless feet of nomads

my love growls softly slow into a child
or a knot of long-legged affirmations
tranquil & ray-banned like ancestor khoisan
against the boiling wiles of the sun
that is silent like the battered death
that sleeps on the skeleton coast
      Mugu ndiye ajua kila kitu
        the elders say

     God is the one who knows everything
     God is the one who knows everything

a roses for the folks we know

now i sing again
too red, the whips flake off my voice
the heart above all things
lechers too many swamps
pure pillars of unpurged babel salt
define the scarred landscape of my heart

but
the songs maul their scanty silences
fire scuttles inward over cities
cursed with forgetful walls

out of every fang a gust of love
out of every fissure seas of welcome
out of every multiplication of howls
a sprawl of sungrass singing repose

a million babygreen roses for the grace
that cushioned the unpillowed silences
between dark & dawn
a million sunblue roses for the sisterknots
of seekers singers & supplicants
whose handshaking supple cordial
hallelujahs the Lord forever
as my dungeons learn windows
seven million roses for the pikin majesties
free from philosophical corrosions
free from hate's biting smite
free from the reckless scalpels of thought

outside the city
the walls fling their profanities ever higher
immune to visions & rainbows
impervious to the ethereal epiphanies
that splinter affliction
oblivious to the thudding spirits
of incoming saints

roses for the glory
roses for the power
roses for the amens
roses for the gifts of the spirit
roses for the untangled dreams
seven million roses for the eternal oil
that surnames every togetherness
seven billion roses for the patient mountain
seven billion roses for the amiable desert
when all we could offer was one foot

for the mothers
who learned very early on
to drink from the muddy wells
between our toes
twelve million roses scented with blessings

for the sisters
who let the wind sleep in their mouths
who let madness sleep under their armpits
who let anguish grow from their gardens
twelve billion roses full of rains...

news riots in from the city
they tell us the walls are falling
with naked indulgences loaded onto their chariots
the heathens gallop south to shallow air
yet still
not enough gallopen roar
will sever the rose's sovereignty—
a rose for you
& for the long road
full of narrownesses
& the straggle of pilgrims

aambl

again it's love that sweeps me in
urgently stancing me into the whirl of the seasons
with their inevitable rainbows or weals
above my anguish that dances on
with the tenacity of a drought
the moon comes out to play
        as it shd
& calls at us in half forgotten languages

i go on singing of those who die & are dead
& won't have rains growing out of their defeated mouths
i go on singing of those who slip in the mud
& immediately holler to the green skies in their hearts
because that is where the hymns pile up
like weary storms that suddenly become contrite

i go on singing of you
who are wasted into a sigh & a dream of rebirths
because the rocks arrogantly insist on being rocks
& not suns or embraces or beginnings
so our home can be in the ancient boulder
that rolls overhead, softly from truth to truth
asserting the slow eternity of all
who dream of pastures & songs

soon the wounds will start looking
like people we know
soon the yells will remind us of unknown loves
soon the forests will be dancing into our screams
& those of us who refuse to forget
their names or strengths
will take over the altars & the skies

sol/o

my love
there are no accidents
in war—no kisses
on the belligerent lips of crocodiles
no loves greener than
the dancing hearts of children
no reveller jollier than the worm
in columbus's boiling head

there are no songs beautifuller
than the stern indifference of the hills
there are no flowers more clamorous
than the seas of children
home in my little heart

i tell u this
as the sun recedes
into the quaking pinstripe
of my warriors
grinning & vulgar in their muddied dreams
of power

i tell us this love
because the roads
have become hostile

Glossary of words, names and places

afs: derogatory name for black people (short for 'Africans')

Alexandra: Johannesburg township

amaboen: 'boere', or Afrikaners

amakaladi: coloureds

amaphela: cockroaches

Asante: kingdom founded in the seventeenth century in present-day Ghana

Azania: among members of the Black Consciousness and related movements, a name for a free South Africa

Baas: master/boss

Bamako: capital of Mali

Bantu: derogatory term for a black African, at one point one of the 'official' Apartheid terms for black people (originally so-named as a speaker of one of the Bantu languages, but subsequently an ethnic designation)

Bantustan: 'ethnic homelands' established by successive Apartheid governments

Bhambatha (Bambatha): the leader of the 1906 Zulu uprising against the British in Natal

Bonk'abajahile: All those who are in a hurry/Everyone is in a hurry

bwana: Mr

Cabo de Esperancia: Cape of Good Hope

cherie: pretty girl

coolie: derogatory word for an Indian

curry-'n-ruti: South African Indian/Malay dish

curryball: derogatory name for a South African of Indian decent

dagga zol: marijuana cigarette

Dollar: Dollar Brand (Abdullah Ibrahim), South African jazz pianist

donga: eroded gully

dories: Doornfontein, early Johannesburg suburb

Dumile: Dumile Fene, a sculptor of the 1960s, forced into exile

eMalangeni: ancestory through the matrileal line; in cosmological terms, a state of innocence

Fransch, Anton: Umkhonto we Sizwe soldier in the Western Cape in the mid-1980s, killed by police after a siege lasting several hours.

gumba: dance party

gumba-gumba: ghetto-blaster

Isandlwana: site of a battle in which the British were defeated by the Zulus in 1879

ja-baas: yes-master

July Handicap: annual Durban horse race

kaak: shit

kaffir: derogatory word for a black person

Karoo: area of semi-desert in the interior of South Africa

Kgalagadi: the Kalahari Desert

khamba: drinking gourd

khehla: old man

khotla: meeting

kierie: a fighting stick or club

Kleurling: Coloured

Kok, Adam: Adam Kok I, first chief of the Griqua, a group of Khoikhoi and mixed decent, which left the Cape in the late eighteenth century, and gained dominance in the early nineteenth century in the middle Orange River region; Adam Kok III: chief under whom the Griquas were dispossessed of their land in the second half of the nineteenth century

kraal: African homestead

kraalmis: kraal mist

kwela: township pennywhistle music

laager: a circular arrangement of ox-wagons for protection of people or animals, a regular defence of the Afrikaner Voortrekkers

laurentina: beer

Luthuli: Albert Luthuli, President of the ANC (1952–67)

Mahlathini: South African gumba musician

majita: guy, buddy

makapulan: cloth worn by women round the hips

Makarere: Makerere University, Kampala

Makeba, Mariam: South African jazz vocalist

makorokoto: congratulations

malombo: jazz idiom combining traditional rythmes with urban jazz

Mankunku: Mankunku Ngoza, South African saxophonist

Mansa Musa: emperor of Mali (1307–37)

maqabane: comrades

Masekela, Hugh: South African jazz musician
mayibuye Afrika: 'come back, Africa', rallying cry of the ANC
mbaqanga: form of popular music combining African and American jazz
Moeketsi, Kippie: South African jazz saxophanist
Mossi: one of a number of powerful kingdoms founded in the fourteenth century in present-day northern Ghana and Upper Volta
Mshweshwe (Moshweshwe I): founder and first King of Lesotho
myneer: mister
Ndlovu: elephant, also the name of a Zulu clan
O.K. Bazaars: South African chainstore
okapi: knife
oliphant: elephant
otsogile: how are you?
oupa: grandfather
palish 'n makov: porridge and spinach
Pik: Roelof Frederick 'Pik' Botha, South African Foreign Minister under two successive Apartheid governments (1977–94)
porras: derogatory name for Portuguese
prêgo and café com leite: steak sandwich with coffee and milk
Robben Island: infamous prison island within view of Cape Town
rondawel: circular house, usually with a thatch roof
Sasol (Suid Afrikaanse Steenkool, Olie en Gaskorporasie): South Africa's oil-from-coal and chemical producing corporation, sabotaged by ANC operatives in June 1980
Shaka: nineteenth-century Zulu king, considered to be the founder of the Zulu nation. His militarised and centralised state was the most powerful force in south-east Africa during the 1820s.
Sharpeville: township in Gauteng, scene of a massacre in March 1960 in which police fired on crowds protesting against the pass laws
shebeen: illegal bar or drinking den
Songhay: an empire founded in 670 AD in present-day eastern Mali
Sophiatown: legendary township in Johannesburg, destroyed under group areas legislation in the 1950s
Tambo: Oliver Tambo, President of the ANC (1977–91)
Temba, Can: South African jazz musician
Thoko: Thoko Mcinga, popular singer of the late 1960s
tjarra: a derogatory name for a South African of Indian decent
tsena: come in
Tshaka: c.f. Shaka

Umkhonto we Sizwe: 'Spear of the Nation', the armed wing of the
    ANC
Witbooi, Hendrik: leader of the Nama, one of several Khoi-khoi
    groups, in the war against the German colonisation of Namibia

Acknowledgements

Arthur Nortje
All poems from *Dead Roots*, Heinemann (1973); with acknowedgements to
the poet and to the University of South Africa Library.

Mongane Wally Serote
'Hell, well, heaven', 'Ofay-watcher looks back', 'City Johannesburg',
'Alexandra', 'Her name is "Dooti"', 'The three mothers', from *Yakhal
'iinkomo* , Renoster Books, Ad. Donker (1972); 'Night-Time', 'Introit'
from *Tselo*, Ad. Donker (1974); extracts from *No Baby Must Weep* from
No Baby Must Weep, Ad. Donker (1975); 'The long road' from *The Night
Keeps Winking*, Medu Art Ensemble (1982)

Mafika Gwala
'Beyond fences', 'One small boy longs for summer', 'An attempt at
communication', 'Election pincers', 'The jive', 'Gumba, gumba, gumba',
'The children of Nonti', 'Getting off the ride' from *Jol'iinkomo*, Ad.
Donker (1977); 'Bonk'abajahile' from *No More Lullabies*, Ad. Donker
(1982)

Wopko Jensma
'Black bottom stomp', 'In memoriam Ben Zwane', 'In solitary', 'Lemmy
knows two', 'Cry me a river', 'Ring da till', 'Fear freedom' from *Where
White is the Colour, Where Black is the Number*, Ravan Press (1974); 'The
pointless objects riddle', 'Spanner in the what? works', 'Suspect under
section a1 special', 'Somewhere in the middle, Sunday', 'Chant of praise for
the idi amin dada' from *I Must Show You My Clippings*, Ravan Press
(1977); 'Letter to Thelonius', 'Portrait of the artist', 'I come', 'Till no one',
'Blue 2', 'Confidentially yours', 'No dreams', 'In memoriam Akbar
Babool' from *Sing for Our Execution*, Ophir, Ravan Press (1973)

Douglas Livingstone
'The sleep of my lions', 'Vanderdecken', 'One Golgotha' from *Eyes Closed
Against the Sun*, Oxford University Press (1970); 'Giovanni Jacopo
meditates (on aspects of art and love)', 'A morning', 'Wheels' from *A
Rosary of Bone*, David Philip (1975); 'Mpondo's smithy, Transkei', 'Dust',
'The recondite war on women', 'Sonatina of Peter Govender, beached'
from *The Anvil's Undertone*, Ad. Donker (1978); 'A Darwinian preface',
'The Waste Land at Station 14', 'Isipingo', 'Traffic interlude: descent from
the tower' from *A Littoral Zone*, Carrefour Press (1991)

Lionel Abrahams

'Thresholds of tolerance' from *Thresholds of Tolerance*, Bateleur (1975); 'Dry self-portrait', 'Our way of life', "After winter '76', 'Out of illness', 'Don't say it', 'Family man' from *Journal of a New Man*, Ad. Donker (1984); 'A stone stood in her house', 'Spring report', 'Privacy', 'Winter report', 'To Halley's Comet', 'Thoughts on Johannesburg's centenary', 'The writer in sand' from *The Writer in Sand*, Ad. Donker (1988); 'Flesh', 'To the idealistic killers', 'Agnostic's funeral prayer', 'Song for the new order', 'At revolution's end' from *A Dead Tree Full of Live Birds*, Snailpress (1995)

Ingrid de Kok

'To drink its water', 'Shadows behind, before', 'Leavetaking', 'At this resort', 'My father would not show us', 'Dream of a trophy', 'Visitor', 'This thing we learn from others', 'Small passing' from *Familiar Ground*, Ravan Press (1988); 'Transfer', 'Ground wave', 'Still life', 'At the Commission', 'Ecotone', 'Mending', 'My mother's house hold', 'The talking cure', 'Text of necessity', 'Salamander', 'Inner note', 'Stay here' from *Transfer*, Snailpress (1997)

Tatamkhulu Afrika

'Dancing in my city', 'The funeral of Anton Fransch', 'The funeral', 'Hit squad' from *Dark Rider*, Snailpress, Mayibuye (1992); 'Maqabane', 'The fist', 'Sleepless' from *Maqabane*, Mayibuye (1994); 'Glimpse of God', To God' from *Flesh and Flame*, Silk Road (1995); 'Nightrider' from *The Lemon Tree*, Snailpress (1995); 'Queue', 'Respite', 'The accident' from *Turning Points*, Mayibuye (1996)

Karen Press

'This is not a riot policeman', 'She brought home poppies', 'Bird' from *Bird Heart Stoning the Sea*, Buchu Books (1990); 'Hope for refugees', from 'Tiresias in the city of heroes', 'Heart's hunger', 'The man with incomplete words on his roof', 'I who live here, it is I', 'Humus', 'Dispossessed words', 'Reclaiming our land', 'Welcome', Statues', 'This, too', 'Ancestors' from *Home*, Carcanet Press (forthcoming); 'Causality and chance in love', 'The first thirty-seven years', 'Rotten fish' from *Eyes Closed Against the Sun*, Gecko Books (1997)

Seitlhamo Motsapi

All poems from *earthstepper / the ocean is very shallow*, Deep South Publishers (1995)